COLLINS GEM

CASTLES
of Scotland

Elaine Henderson

**With an introduction by
Julian Small**

HarperCollins*Publishers*

HarperCollins Publishers
PO Box, Glasgow G4 0NB

First published 1994
This edition published 1999

Reprint 10 9 8 7 6 5 4 3 2 1 0

All photographs supplied by the Still Moving Picture Company
except on pages: 29, 33, 37, 43, 45, 49, 57, 63, 73, 81, 87, 105,
109, 117, 119, 123, 135, 145, 157, 161, 169, 171, 175, 179, 181,
183, 195, 211 – Historic Scotland; 9, 129, 147, 153, 155, 159
– Royal Commission on the Ancient and Historical Monuments
of Scotland; 7, 137 – The Edinburgh Photographic Library;
113, 167 – Marius Alexander Photography; 43 – David Whyte;
141 – Doug Corrance; 55 – Stuart Morris of Balgonie; 201 –
National Trust for Scotland.

Line drawings on pages 16, 41 and 47 by Roy Boyd

ISBN 0 00 472266-3

Printed in Italy by Amadeus S.p.A.

❈ CONTENTS ❈

THE HISTORY OF FORTIFICATIONS
IN SCOTLAND

The castle is always seen as being a typically Scottish building type. The laird living in his castle is regarded as being as typical of Scotland as the squire in his manor house is of England. And, more than most such generalizations, this has a large element of truth in it: very many Scottish lairds do live in castles – or in castle-like buildings. And the vision conjured up by this description, that of a tall building with small windows and with pepper-pot turrets – bartizans, as they are properly known – at the corners of the parapet, is the picture gained by many visitors to Scotland. The vast majority of Scottish castles visible today are of 16th- or 17th-century date (and there are even more imitations of the type built during the 19th century than there are originals); these often replace earlier castles nearby or on the same site, and the study of the structures of different dates has so much to tell us about the different ways people lived at different times.

Properly, of course, the castle is closely defined. It possesses a dual nature: it is both a domestic residence and a fortress; equally importantly, it is a product of the feudal system of government (feudalism). Feudalism was a system based on land tenure, in which the king granted lands to his followers in return for military service. These tenants-in-chief (those who held land directly of the king) might grant land on similar terms to so-called sub-tenants. The peasants, or clansmen in the Highlands, promised to follow their lord, whether tenant-in-chief or sub-tenant, and fight in his service (or, alternatively, in more fully developed feudal systems, provided the labour on the lord's estate). All land was therefore considered as belonging to the king and was held by his subjects in return for services due ultimately to the king. The system was never fully implemented in Scotland, but the descendants of St Margaret saw its advantages and took any opportunity to extend its operation during a period which saw quite extensive changes in landholding.

We must not forget, however, that castles were also places where people lived as well as defensive structures: both aspects influenced their architecture as well as their nature. They were not the empty shells that many are today, or the large family homes that they are when still inhabited, but, however like or unlike our expectations of a 'castle', all the examples quoted are well worth visiting and spending some time getting to know.

EARTHWORK CASTLES

Earthwork castles, as found in Scotland, tend to be one of three types: ringworks, mottes and motte-and-bailey castles. None of these types is plentiful, but the motte-and-bailey is probably the most widely found.

The ringwork is probably the least frequently recognized of these three types of earthwork castle. It was, as its name suggests, no more than a ditch dug around a lordly or other residence. The material dug out was used to form a bank immediately within the ditch, the bank being topped, it is believed, by a wooden palisade or stockade. The buildings enclosed within the courtyard would most likely be of timber initially, but as time went on, some of them might be replaced in stone. This form developed into the earliest stone-walled castles, such as Castle

Sween, during the late 12th century. Ringworks built on good soil but subsequently abandoned have very likely been taken into cultivation and the earthwork of bank and ditch ploughed away. If the site has been in continuous occupation or has been refortified, the earliest remains have almost certainly been replaced and almost obliterated by later work in stone. Amongst the finest examples remaining is the apparent ringwork surrounding the 15th-century Crookston Castle. If this is, as it seems, of the late 12th century, then the ditch and bank, which enclose over an acre, would have surrounded a group of timber buildings. The bank, originally topped by a wooden palisade, seems to have been broken by only the one entrance, on the west side. All traces of buildings within the courtyard have disappeared, but the size of the enclosed area shows the status originally accorded the site.

The motte-and-bailey castle and the motte are, as is obvious from the terms, related forms. Motte, which comes from the French word for 'mound', is just that: a large earthen mound with sufficient space on top for a tower. When built, the tower (like all the structures of the motte-and-bailey castle) would have been of wood. The bailey was the courtyard at the base of the motte – sometimes, but not always, on a lower mound of its own, as at the highly impressive remains of Inverurie Castle – housing the service buildings of the castle, and, like the ringwork, surrounded by a ditch and a wooden palisade. The tower on the motte, the most secure point, was generally the residence of the lord and his family, and it would also have been used as a lookout point. Accommodation for the lord's followers, together with stables, storehouses and a great hall for communal meals, would have been in the bailey. It should also be remembered that the castle was — like the country house of later centuries — the centre for an agricultural estate, and although the work on it was done by the peasantry, the lord farmed the demesne land (the word has been preserved in corrupted form in many places in Scotland as 'Mains'); barns and storehouses formed an essential part of any castle.

To protect these, the motte and the bailey would both be surrounded by timber palisades and by a deep (possibly as much as 16 feet/five metres) and wide ditch. On hilltops this would be dry, but on lower-lying ground it could be water-filled; frequently, existing streams or boggy areas would be utilized in the defences.

A motte

In a number of cases — as, for example, at the Peel-Ring of Lumphanan — mottes were present without a bailey. If this was the case, the motte would need to be able to accommodate on its top all the accommodation normally housed in both motte and bailey. It therefore needed to be a wide-topped mound.

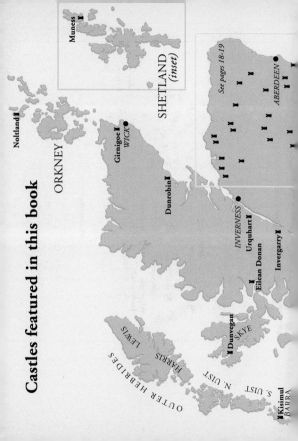

Castles featured in this book

ORKNEY

SHETLAND *(inset)*

Muness

Noltland

Girnigoe • WICK

Dunrobin

See pages 18–19

ABERDEEN •

• INVERNESS

Urquhart

Invergarry

Eilean Donan

OUTER HEBRIDES

LEWIS

HARRIS

N. UIST

S. UIST

Dunvegan SKYE

Kisimul BARRA

Dunnottar ✝
Edzell ✝

Glamis ✝

Blair ✝
Castle Menzies ✝

FORT WILLIAM
✝ Dunstaffnage

✝ Inveraray

✝ Carnasserie

✝ Castle Sween
Rothesay ✝
Skipness ✝
Lochranza ✝

MULL
Duart ✝

JURA

ISLAY

See pages 32–33

DUNDEE ✝ ✝
✝ ✝
✝
PERTH ✝
✝
✝ ✝
STIRLING ✝
✝
✝ ✝
GLASGOW ✝
✝

Dumbarton ✝
✝ Newark
✝ Crookston
Kelburn ✝
✝ Brodick

ARRAN

AYR
✝ Culzean
✝ Loch Doon

Dundonald ✝

EDINBURGH
✝
✝ ✝
✝

BERWICK-UPON-TWEED

✝ Thirlestane
PEEBLES ✝
✝ Neidpath ✝ Smailholm ✝ Floors

✝ Drumlanrig ✝ Hermitage
✝ Morton
DUMFRIES ✝ Lochmaben
✝ Comlongan
✝ Caerlaverock

NEWTON STEWART
✝ Threave
Carsluith ✝ ✝ Cardoness
Lochnaw ✝ ✝ ✝ MacLellan's
Castle

The vast majority of mottes in Scotland seem to have been formed from, or at least based upon, natural hillocks; obviously, adapting a natural hill produced a much more stable mound. Mottes, however, were built to take timber towers and if these were succeeded by stone replacements — even allowing time for the motte to stabilize — the mound still might not support the great weight of stone structures.

Castles with mottes are clustered in particular areas of Scotland. Practically none are found in the Lothians, which were close to the centres of authority in the Anglo-Norman kingdom; however, large numbers are to be found in Moray and they are particularly heavily clustered in Galloway. It cannot be a coincidence that these were the peripheral areas being brought under central, royal control during the two centuries of the Anglo-Norman kingdom. Motte-and-bailey castles could be quickly and easily built, and, as in early Norman England, were an ideal form of stronghold for landowners living under 'frontier' conditions. The dates provided in these areas by excavation are all of the 13th century, with occupation in many cases continuing into the period of the Wars of Independence or Wars with England at the very end of that century and beginning of the next. The important point is that motte-and-bailey castles are most common in turbulent areas: England during the 13th century, and central Scotland under the kings of the Canmore dynasty, were relatively peaceful and untroubled areas, and — apart from display of status or the occasional strategic need — there was no requirement to build castles (and certainly not quickly-constructed and hence obviously functional castles); Galloway and Moray were not peaceful, and so had that need.

This is not to say that all motte-and-bailey castles are of such late date; the remains of Inverurie Castle, for example, are dated to the 1170s. But it is important to realize that there was no change of dynasty in Scotland during the 11th century and, in contrast to England, the Norman infiltration was gradual and peaceful so that there was not the same need to construct castles.

EARLY STONE CASTLES

There is no aspect of castle building in Scotland equivalent to the building of the great stone keeps like Falaise in Normandy or like Dover or Norwich in England. However, the alternative to providing a free-standing keep was for one of the towers attached to the enclosing wall – the curtain wall – to play a similar role, with self-contained defences, and in 13th-century Scotland this was the normal pattern. Such a donjon, as it was termed, could not be as secure as a free-standing keep, but it served the same function in that the defenders could, in theory, withdraw there if the main defences of the castle were breached. The donjon can be recognized in an early castle, as the tower will be larger, and probably taller, than the other towers, placed in the least accessible part of the site, and might, for example, control access to the parapets. As well as acting as the final refuge during any siege of the castle, the donjon was intended to be the residence of the lord and his family: the high quality of the detail in the apartments in the donjon at Bothwell Castle is testimony to this, and the same can be seen at Dirleton.

In its ancestry, such a castle, known as a 'castle of enceinte' (literally, castle of enclosure) or courtyard castle, owed more to the ringwork of the 12th century than to the motte-and-bailey.

In the north and particularly the west of Scotland a few early castles, built as stone versions of the ringwork, survive. The most obvious example of this class is the circular Rothesay Castle, built as the very close equivalent to the shell keep found in England and elsewhere (although in England usually on a motte) – a circular wall with lightly-constructed buildings against its inner side

Some other castles were relatively simple constructions, too. Castle Sween is often considered to be the earliest remaining castle of enceinte, but its simple lines were echoed at other examples. Balvenie Castle, a stronghold of the Comyns, was also constructed as a square stone enclosure with the accommodation – of a very basic nature – built against the inner side of the enclosing walls. These buildings would have included a great hall, accommodation for the Lord and his family (although it is possible that a tower existed at one corner which might have acted as a donjon), together with accommodation for the household, and also storehouses and service buildings such as stables. It has even been suggested that Balvenie had towers at all four corners, like the castle of the other branch of the Comyn family at Lochindorb, but at most this must be said to be 'not proven'. It is, however, true that the layout of Lochindorb bears a startling resemblance to that of Inverlochy Castle, held by the same branch of the Comyns: they are even of relatively similar dimensions. In both, once again, the accommodation – apart from that in the towers – would have been in ranges around the courtyard and was of such light construction that few traces remain above ground. The original accommodation would have been similar to that described for Balvenie.

Activity would have centred on the great hall. The hall provided the main eating place, and for many the main sleeping place. At what was termed the 'lower' end of the hall, was the outside entrance, placed in the side wall, and giving access to a screens passage or transe, a passage running across the building (an attempt to divert draughts from blowing through into the main room); from here, access was gained on one side to the lower end of the hall, and on the other, very frequently to the kitchen. At the far end of the hall from the screen was the high table, which might stand on a dais, and – more importantly in terms of understanding the layout – the entrance to the lord's accommodation. This might be

Inverlochy, a 13th-century courtyard castle

in a tower projecting to one side, as at Lochranza Castle, in a block forming a continuation of the hall range, as at Hailes Castle, or, if the hall was located in the donjon, as at Bothwell Castle and at Inverlochy Castle, on the floor above. In many motte-and-bailey castles the lord's accommodation would be on the motte, the most secure part of the castle, rather than leading off the hall, but his life would remain centred on the hall, using the security and privacy of the motte-top quarters at night. Some of the household – the inhabitants of a castle comprised far more than the lord and his family and soldiers to defend it, but a whole community of servants and members of the household – would sleep in the hall, but there must have been other quarters for some of them: it was not an age of much personal privacy, but there would be sufficient accommodation to give some degree of privacy to those members of the household who carried some status. Guests would be housed according to their rank, eating in the hall either at the lord's table or one of the lower tables and sleeping anywhere from the lord's own solar or private chamber down to a cloak on the hall floor with the ordinary members of the household.

Quite apart from castles proper, there can be found in Scotland a group of fortified houses termed 'hall houses', in other words fortified and defensible free-standing halls, surrounded by a defensive palisaded bank. Essentially, they are of the same form as the ringworks of the 12th century, but with the main hall rebuilt in stone. A number of hall houses have ben recognized in western Scotland (for example, the one only thinly disguised by 16th-century alteration at Lochranza on Arran), but the type is spread throughout the country, for example at

14

Aberdour and Hailes, with others no doubt awaiting identification elsewhere.

Hall houses are more analogous to medieval manor houses in England than to English castles, and they reflect the settled conditions of peace with England and a strong monarchy during the 13th century. At the same time, there exists in the more settled, central areas of Scotland, a group of extremely impressive and strongly fortified castles, showing an up-to-date knowledge of military theory and developments in military technology. They demonstrate a development (paralleling that elsewhere in Britain) from the conventional reliance on a curtain wall with towers at the angles, trying to defend the whole circuit of walls, as found at Buittle Castle or the early remains at Eilean Donan, to a castle where the emphasis lay on defence from the gatehouse, such as can be found at Kildrummy or Caerlaverock Castles. The entrance to the castle was always its weakest point, and so from a simple gate developed the gatehouse, to try to defend that weak point: drawbridge, portcullis and machicolations (openings from an over-hanging parapet from which defenders could drop missiles on to attackers) were relatively early developments; barbicans (foreworks to protect the gate and prevent attackers from reaching it, as at Inverlochy Castle) were later embellishments. But as greater emphasis was placed on the defence of the gate, gatehouses became more elaborate, until the stage of Caerlaverock Castle (where the major part of the accommodation was formed in the gatehouse), or the very sophisticated gatehouse of Kildrummy Castle was reached. Over the same period, other elements of the defences had also developed, for example arrow slits, which although they never

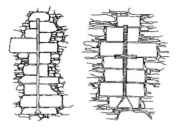

Arrow slits:
simple slit (far left);
cross shape (left)

reached the heights of elaboration sometimes found in England or Wales, developed from simple slits (as can be seen at Dunstaffnage Castle) to cross shapes (as found at Bothwell Castle) in order to give the archer visibility over a wider field. The wide embrasures in the wall behind the slit allowed the archer some cover from any attackers. The inspiration for the new forms of defences, gatehouses included, came both from England and France. Excavations at Dundonald Castle show that the early castle possessed two gigantic gatehouses on diagonally-opposite corners of the castle, which seems to have had a very similar plan to that of Rhuddlan Castle, North Wales. Rhuddlan, of course, had been built during Edward I's campaigns against the Welsh, so Dundonald was quick to develop the idea before being destroyed during the Wars with England. For Edward I had now turned his attention northwards, and the 'Hammer of the Scots', after capturing Berwick-on-Tweed in March 1296, involved himself in the long, bitter struggle to try to extend his hold over the northern kingdom, a war which, before its culmination at Bannockburn in

1314, had turned England from a co-operative neighbour and friendly rival to 'the Auld Enemy'.

TOWER HOUSES AND ALTERNATIVES TO TOWER HOUSES

The transformation of England from the cousins on the other side of the border to the 'Auld Enemy' marked an end to English architectural influence. From now on, developments might be paralleled, and some influence might come indirectly (contacts with Ireland continued strong in the west), but Scotland now looked in particular to France for architectural inspiration, as she did politically, and also, increasingly, to the Low Countries and other trading partners across the North Sea, or concentrated on developing Scottish native traditions and home-grown architectural forms.

During the Wars with England, Robert I ordained a policy of slighting castles – that is, partially destroying the defences so as to render them useless to the enemy as strongholds, should they be captured, without major rebuilding. The Scots had no access to the sort of siege engines possessed by King Edward, and it was consequently much more difficult for the Scots to recapture castles taken by the English than it was for the English to capture them in the first place. Construction of fortifications was very limited while the constant English invasions continued under King Robert and his son, David II. When building interest gradually turned once again to castles, it took a completely different form to what had gone before in Scotland: the tower house.

NAIRN

Cawdor

Brodie

Darnaway

Duffus

Spynie

KEITH

Ballindalloch

Balvenie

Spey

Glenbuchat

CAIRNGORMS

Braemar

Balmoral

Castles in the Northeast

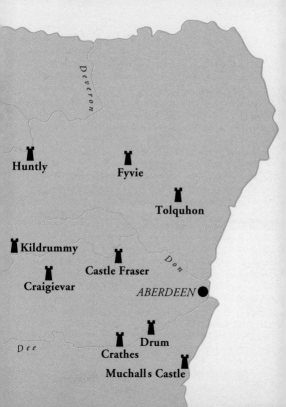

One of the few buildings with which the name of Robert I is associated is Tarbert Castle in Kintyre. Here, in 1325, the king ordered the repair and enlargement of an existing royal castle to act as a strongpoint in what was, and always had been, a restive area. The slight remains seem to show King Robert's work taking the form of a large bailey, with drum, or round towers attached to the outer side at intervals around the circuit. The courtyard was too immense for everyday use, but it is tempting to speculate that it was intended to form a mustering point for the royal army should it be needed. Essentially, the work at Tarbert is in the 13th-century tradition. More typical of castles built in the aftermath of the Wars with England is Dundonald Castle, where the replacement for the 13th-century castle not only took the form of a tower (albeit one of unusual form and on an unusually substantial scale for its date), but the tower was built over the site of, and incorporated fragments from, one of the two gatehouses of its predecessor. Although the earlier walls must have been standing to quite a substantial height, the new tower ignored them by absorbing them, the two round towers (the gate between them blocked) projecting from the wall like beached whales. The remains of the earlier castle had no relevance to the builders of the tower house.

Scotland may never have known the great stone keeps found throughout 12th-century Europe, but the late medieval tower house, generally regarded as the classic Scottish castle, has sometimes been seen as their equivalent. This flexible form was adopted during the mid-14th century (although the earliest examples are not securely dated and might even be as early as the end of the 13th century), and was developed by continued use, elaborated when occasion required, and persisted as the normal form for a laird's residence until the early 17th century. The resemblance to the 12th-century keep may be misleading, as the two types function in very different ways, but the persistent popularity of the tower house as a building type bears witness to the fact that late medieval Scottish society was as unsettled as that of the rest of northern Europe. Nevertheless, three hundred years of development, and three hundred years of experimentation with internal layout, made the tower house an increasingly sophisticated structure.

Many tower houses were built on the same sites which had attracted the builders of mottes, equally, many were on new sites with the sites of earlier castles abandoned. The dangers of erecting stone towers on the top of earlier mottes has already been mentioned, in some cases the stone buildings proving be too heavy for the largely artificial motte. In many cases, however, mottes were successfully reused.

Tower houses reflect the way of life of their occupants, thus, although they may vary in details, they tend more than many types of building to follow a similar basic design. Once, as a visitor, you understand the functions of the various parts, it is easy to work out how the parts fit together in any individual tower house. Early tower houses demonstrate the pattern of life very aptly: the ground floor formed a storage basement, usually capped by a stone vault; above this was the hall (a more lofty room than the others and also frequently vaulted); above the hall was the laird's chamber (the solar); and finally there may be further accommodation beneath the roof, in the so-called garret. The earliest tower houses may have up to three vaults, one above another, but during the 15th century it became more common for only the basement (and sometimes not even that) to be vaulted. It is also very common to find that a vaulted storey has corbels or joist pockets (beam holes) halfway up the walls: this is a sign that there was an entresol or mezzanine floor, sometimes entered separately from the turnpike stair, sometimes entered by a ladder leading up from the main floor level.

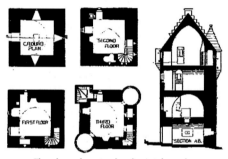

Floor plans and a section through a typical tower house

Most early tower houses were entered at first-floor level, although in later examples a ground-floor entrance is more common. Cawdor Castle is an example of a tower which has always been inhabited and where, for convenience the first-floor entrance has been blocked (although it is very obvious to see) and entry brought down to ground level. This disturbs the whole pattern of circulation within the tower, for all tower houses are designed to provide security in a particular way: access is at one end of the hall, either from a first-floor entrance or via a stair (either straight or a turnpike) from the basement; access to the upper floors may well be by a separate stair to that connecting with the basement, very frequently rising from the far end of the hall, so that any intruder would face as difficult a task as possible in gaining access to the upper floors. Convenience of circulation within the castle was sacrificed to security.

Although security was a major consideration in the design and construction of tower houses, most of them should not be seen as intended to withstand a fully-pressed siege. The great castles of enceinte of the 13th century had been designed with that in mind, but tower houses developed as a result of royal policy of discouragement of castle building; they could not be held against the king, either by their owners or by the English enemy should they invade. But in an unpoliced society strong walls, a walled courtyard, and all the paraphernalia of defence which a tower house could display, although of little use against an attacking army prepared to sit out a siege, would deter marauders, whether from a rival clan, a feuding family, or raiders from over the border. The early Stewart kings were not strong leaders, and the general insecurity was only exacerbated during the 15th century by a succession of early royal deaths followed by long periods of regency on behalf of child kings. Wars with England occurred spasmodically, and there were struggles between Crown and nobility, notably with the Douglases. Such political instability meant that the wise man looked for some form of physical security.

Only with the introduction of small pieces of artillery during the second half of the 15th century (until this time, possession of artillery was almost a royal prerogative), and the subsequent introduction of handheld guns, was there a radical change in the nature of tower house defence, as gunloops were built to take advantage of the new weapon. With gunloops, defence took place from the lower storeys of the tower house. The fact that until then, defence was conducted from wall-head level, in the same way as in most of the early west-coast castles, suggests that in neither case was there any expectation of having to withstand a fully-pressed siege. Nevertheless, although resistance to a large attacking force was almost certain to be futile, a surprising number of tower houses appear to have undergone sieges.

The tower house was almost ubiquitous in Scotland. All the landowning class, from the king downwards, built them, and few indeed are the other forms of accommodation in castles until the 16th century. The earliest and simplest tower houses were square – for example those at Drum and at Lochleven. The former seems to date to the early 14th century but shows many of the typical features of the later tower house in embryo, and the latter presents a number of very archaic-looking features, such as the lack of the overhanging parapets present even at Drum. The early examples possess either a stair ascending in a single flight within the thickness of the wall – a mural stair – or a slightly thickened wall at the corner to accommodate a spiral. Although Drum and Lochleven are early and hence relatively unsophisticated, later square or rectangular towers such as at Spynie Palace or Elphinstone Castle, East Lothian (now largely demolished due to mining subsidence), had their walls

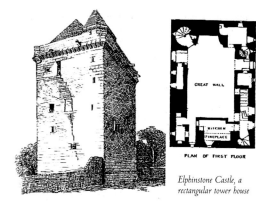

Elphinstone Castle, a rectangular tower house

elaborately hollowed out to form galleries and chambers on a variety of different levels, not necessarily related to the main floor levels of the tower. This should be seen as demonstrating the same approach to design as can be seen in the more complicated L- and Z-plan towers, that a tower house does not possess horizontal suites of rooms, one to each floor, but is treated as a series of vertical ranges, or even suites, of rooms, one above another, reached by separate stairs – in other words, a series of parallel towers: the hall and chamber block of such a 13th-century hall house as Morton Castle or the early work at Skipness Castle upended.

This concept can be more easily understood from L-plan towers than from the rectangular towers adopting part of the same technique. In some cases the jamb, or wing, of the 'L' housed the staircase, or part of the staircase – either that from the hall upward, or more usually (because it also frequently housed the entrance) from the ground floor up. But if it were the former, and there were also rooms in the jamb, they tended to be entered separately from the stair, with floor levels unrelated to those in the main part of the tower – an aspect which can be seen, for example, at Craigmillar Castle.

The great advantage of the L-plan tower house over the rectangular was the ability to provide cover (from wallhead level, of course, until the introduction of gunloops), not only along two of the walls, but also – and more importantly – for the entrance to the tower, which is in this case almost invariably in the re-entrant angle of the jamb. The tower house may have been little more than minimally defensible, but providing effective cover for the entrance went a long way towards making the defences effective.

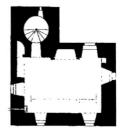

Carsluith Castle, an L-plan tower house

The L-plan tower house was an early development from the rectangular. The earliest known example was that built by King David II at Edinburgh Castle and firmly documented to 1367-1379. Its remains are today invisible, the ruins left after the bombardment of 1573 being buried within the Half-Moon Battery. But this is proof indeed that the tower house was the accepted form of accommodation for even the highest in the land, and at one of the most important royal castles: a tower house, once of rare elaboration, seemingly containing both King's and Queen's apartments – hall and chamber in each case – on separate storeys in a high, large and strong tower. It is generally suggested that this was indeed the very first L-plan tower, with all others being inspired by the very practical example set by royalty.

It was some further time, however, before the most fully developed plan-type, the Z-plan, was added to the architectural vocabulary as yet another form which could be used for a laird's house (although rectangular and L-plan towers remained popular). In the Z-plan form, towers are attached to two, diagonally-opposed, corners of the main block. These towers can both be square, both round (rooms within round towers may be round, square or polygonal), or – no less common than the other variations – one of each. It enables all four walls of the main block (and the vulnerable re-entrant angles) to receive covering fire in case of attack. In addition, and probably more important still, it allowed an increase in accommodation, and in the more settled Scotland of the reign of James VI, that increase was often greatly desired.

As well as being probably the most sophisticated castle-form

Glenbuchat Castle, a Z-plan tower house with square towers

in Scotland, the Z-plan was a relatively late development. The type apparently originated in the northeast of Scotland, probably in Aberdeenshire, and remained particularly popular there. The earliest example identified is the great tower built at Huntly, constructed during the 1550s. No other example dates from before the Reformation of 1560, and it has been suggested that the second attached tower at Huntly is not of the same date as the rest of the block, which incorporates work of several periods. It was, as work to Castle Fraser suggests, quite a straightforward matter to extend an L-plan tower to a Z-plan. Even when the two towers are of the same date — as can be seen at Carnasserie Castle or Elcho Castle — there will usually be separate stairs for the two. The apartments of the laird and his family were isolated from those of the visitors, allowing a greater degree of privacy for the laird, and rather more control over circulation within the tower.

By the late 16th century tower houses had developed further. Not only was a far greater degree of comfort expected, but there was an increasing desire to impress the visitor with the laird's status by means of architectural elaboration. For almost the first time we can begin to identify the work of individual master masons, such as that of the anonymous masons who worked at both Carnasserie Castle and at Torwood Castle, near Stirling. Sometimes it is possible to put names to them, most notably with the Bell family of masons in Aberdeenshire, who together worked on the exceptionally beautiful and interesting group of castles comprising Crathes, Fyvie, Fraser, Midmar and Craigievar. Likewise, the castles built on Orkney and Shetland by the Stewart Earls of Orkney, including Muness, Scalloway, and the later work at Noltland, seem to be the product of one mind, possibly that of Andrew Crawford, Master of Work to Earls Robert and Patrick; these, too, are very accomplished pieces of design.

What must not be forgotten is that the tower house, whether square tower or any of the variations of form, never stood alone but always within a barmkin, or courtyard, which contained other buildings. As much as the castles of enceinte, the tower house would have been the centre of an agricultural estate, part of it farmed directly, and in addition to such buildings as stables, barns and storehouses would also be required. More than this the barmkin, as is only now being recognized, contained a great deal of further accommodation for members of the laird's household other than his family. The recent excavation of the barmkin at Smailholm Tower has demonstrated that even for a relatively minor lairdish household there was a need for rather more accommodation than was provided within the tower, including a second hall for the lesser members of the household.

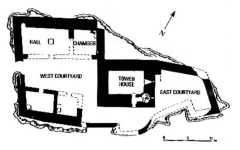

HALL □ CHAMBER

WEST COURTYARD

TOWER HOUSE

EAST COURTYARD

N

*Plan of Smailholm Tower, showing the courtyard
buildings in the 16th century*

The barmkin buildings were usually of much lighter construction than the walls of the main tower, in many cases possibly of wood, and in most cases have totally vanished. In later times in many castles the barmkin buildings were gradually rebuilt in more substantial fashion, as in the many different phases of work which have been identified around the courtyard of Crichton Castle, or more completely rebuilt, as at Drum or Eilean Donan. But they, or their predecessors, will once have existed around every tower house, however isolated it may seem to stand today.

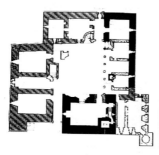

*Plan of Crichton Castle,
showing the courtyard
surrounded by buildings
of different dates*

────── KEY ──────
black area: *late 14thC*
grey area: *about 1450*
white area: *about 1585*

True courtyard castles also existed in late medieval Scotland,
although the popularity of the tower house with all social classes
meant that they are few and far between, and many of those
which did exist were refortifications of earlier castles. Bothwell,
Urquhart, Spynie and Kildrummy come under the latter
heading, and it is interesting – and perhaps significant – that at
the second and third of these, tower houses were constructed
within the enclosures to provide the main accommodation during the later period. By contrast, Tantallon was built by the
Douglases without a tower house, but it acted as a
demonstration of the power and wealth drawn from their lands
in East Lothian, as much as to guard the entrance to the Firth of
Forth. However, the flexibility of the tower house, and its
universal popularity with the land-owning classes in Scotland,
ensured that Tantallon was very much the exception rather than
the rule.

31

Claypotts

DUNDEE

Huntingtower

PERTH Megginch

Elcho

Falkland

Burleigh Loch Leven

Doune

Menstrie Castle Campbell

Stirling Ravenscraig

Balgonie

FIRTH

Aberdour

Rough

Blackness Lauriston

Niddry

Edinburgh

Craigmillar

Bothwell

Craignethan

Broughty

Castles in the
Edinburgh/Fife area

. Andrews

Kellie

F FORTH

Tantallon

Dirleton

Dunbar

Hailes

Crichton

Ayton

BERWICK-UPON-TWEED ●

The most ambitious architectural campaigns of the early 16th century are those of the royal castles and palaces. Quite apart from the very substantial work at Linlithgow and Holyroodhouse, James IV and James V contributed largely to what we see today at Edinburgh and Stirling Castles, and reconstructed Falkland Palace. The work at Stirling, particularly, is of tremendous significance. Stirling was a favourite residence of nearly all the Stewart dynasty, and work here, in particular, was intended to provide a properly regal setting for majesty, and to try to impress upon visiting dignitaries that the King of Scots was a prince to rank with any in Europe. The Great Hall at Stirling, built by James IV around 1500 as a formal setting for all manner of royal ceremonies, is undeniably impressive today, and must have been far more so when first built.

As an equally impressive introduction to the regal splendour of the Parliament Hall, as the Stirling hall is often called, James IV also reconstructed the main entrance to the castle, the Forework, work which was probably carried out during the first decade of the 16th century, very likely following immediately upon completion of the hall. This was once again intended to impress visitor and subject alike, with an approximately symmetrical facade. Even now, with the gatehouse reduced in height during the 18th century and with other parts altered or destroyed, it forms a magnificent entrance to the Lower Square.

James IV's son, James V, also embellished Stirling. During the 1540s he gave a great deal of his attention to the building of the so-called Palace block (the new royal apartments), replacing buildings which were themselves only constructed by his father. The attempt to create a Renaissance-style palace came about as a result of his employment of French masons, and even though in the execution of the work by Scottish masons a number of very Scottish accents have crept in, the importance of this work must be realized. It was amongst the earliest efforts to provide classical facades in Britain, and this is echoed in the sculptural details. The interior decoration was equally splendid, and although much has now disappeared, enough can be seen to give an impression of the original splendour.

ROMANTIC CASTLES

The apparent lack of major building projects, apart from the royal palaces, during the first half of the 16th century is now being demonstrated to be an illusion. Many of the romantic castles of the late 16th and early 17th centuries are remodellings of those built during the first half of the 16th century, but traditionally ascribed to the later date because of dates carved on the remodelled work. Some work of the early 16th century does survive unaltered, however, and it shows a style of transition. The Reformation, and the redistribution in ownership of land which it brought about, together with the establishment of peace during the more settled reign of James VI (following the struggles of the reign of Queen Mary and James VI's minority), saw a change in emphasis in the second half of the century. From this period onwards, the needs of defence gradually gave way before the desire to build on a more expansive – and frequently expensive – scale. Buildings such as the range constructed at Crichton Castle during the 1580s, with windows looking outwards, are quite unprecedented until James VI's reign. Walls became thinner, dormer windows along wall-heads (as seen, for example, at Newark Castle) frequently replace crenellated parapets and machicolations. Scale-and-platt stairs (like that at Crichton) replace turnpikes.

And yet, despite all this, Scottish lairds continued to build using an essentially castle-like style, and it was not until the mid 17th century that country houses, as known in England, began to be built. It seems obvious that, to these lairds, the feeling was that gentlemen should live in castles. In addition, there was a nostalgic interest in chivalry, and it is actually not so surprising that, while Sir Charles Cavendish should be building a sham castle at Bolsover in Derbyshire, and other sham castles were being built throughout England and Wales, Scottish masons should have continued to build castles. There was, after all, much more reason in Scotland to be concerned about defensibility, with such unsettled conditions in the recent past.

Elcho Castle illustrates this very well. Elcho was constructed as an exceptionally fine tower house, with every attention paid to comfort within, and, indeed, a very sophisticated lay-out. It had a medium-sized barmkin, with a tower remaining at one corner. But although the barmkin wall is obviously intended to deter, and the windows all still have the grilles intended to exclude the intruder or attacker, Elcho was never intended to defy more serious threats. But, to provide some effect of deterrence and impressiveness, it was given a fantastic and romantic roofline. In the tradition of tower houses, the main walls were relatively plain, with elaboration concentrated at parapet level, but the dramatic skyline it presents seems intentionally romantic.

A late 16th-century romantic skyline, Castle Fraser

The same tendency had been reflected in France some years earlier, at such buildings as the Chateaux of Chambord and Azay-le-Rideau, and more recently in England at Wollaton Hall, Nottinghamshire, and in Wales at Ruperra Castle, Glamorgan. In Scotland, it particularly affected those few castles which were now beginning to be built to a courtyard plan. Tolquhon is a case in point, where the gatehouse range, with decorative gunloops, is playfully martial. Tolquhon, as do most examples of the romantic style, makes more than just a play of defensiveness: there are no sizeable external windows on the ground floor; in addition to the decorative gunloops at the outer gate, there are practical ones, as well, covering all the strategic points; and there is only one external entrance to the castle courtyard. Here the old tower was not incorporated into the principal accommodation, but a new, tall block 'reads' as being

37

the laird's tower, and the old tower was retained only as subsidiary accommodation. This continued stress laid on the tower demonstrates an underlying desire for security, although it was a very different type of tower, with the rooms frequently arranged in horizontal suites, as for example at Huntly Castle, rather than in vertical sequence. The horizontal suite is much more convenient than the vertical disposition of rooms in the old-fashioned type of tower house such as Castle Craig or Castle Campbell.

It is hardly surprising that there was a general desire to retain some sort of tower. From the perspective of the early 17th century, history had been so turbulent that there was no guarantee that conditions would not soon return to their former state; the wise man, like Lord Nithsdale at Caerlaverock, put not his trust in princes, but built his new mansion as a courtyard range in the security of his moated castle. Lord Nithsdale was, in fact, quite right to be cautious, as Caerlaverock was to play a significant role in the civil war between King and Covenant in 1640.

However, the location of Lord Nithsdale's new lodging in the old castle made no difference to the comfort of the mansion being built, as is made quite clear by the furnishings recorded in an inventory of 1640: it housed five beds, two of silk and three of cloth, ten lesser beds and twenty servants' beds, the furniture of a drawing room uphostered in silver cloth, and a library of books which had cost Lord Nithsdale £200. Lord Nithsdale's mansion is a ruin today, but the splendour of the interiors can be gauged from contemporary castles which remain intact, for example Muchalls with its plastered interiors, or Newark with its panelling.

The introduction of artillery into Scotland during the late 14th century led to a revolution in the defence of tower houses. One of the most conspicuous aspects of tower house design had been that it was defended from wallwalks behind parapets at roof level. Now, for the first time since the 13th century, we see defence carried out from within the building. At first, the new invention was, because of its expense and rarity, a royal prerogative, but it was not long before distribution became more widespread. It was not until the mid-15th century, however, that the implications of artillery began to leave visible architectural traces.

The Stewart kings lavished much attention on their artillery trains, and not least attentive of them was James II (1437-1460). To the struggle for power between him and the powerful Earls of Douglas, we owe the artillery fortification surrounding the tower house of Threave Castle – the earliest in Scotland and one of the earliest in Europe. So effective was it, that after a three-month siege in 1455, the king was forced to resort to a more conventional weapon – bribery of the officers of the garrison! The newly-built fortification that was so successful in frustrating the king's train of artillery, consists of a relatively low wall with drum towers at the angles, built around the two most vulnerable sides of the tower house. Externally, the wall has a batter (slope) to cushion the impact of the shots, and regularly-placed gunloops of early form. These gunloops are unlikely all to have housed guns, but many would have housed the more conventional archers, armed with long-bows and cross-bows.

The first castle to be built – rather than remodelled or adapted – as an artillery fortification was that at Ravenscraig in Fife. It is possible that some of the visible work here dates from a secondary phase, but it is clear even so that the original work, under construction between 1460 and 1463, was intended as an artillery fortification. The gunloops are placed so as to provide enfilading fire and the two towers are so designed as to offer maximum resistance to any attacking artillery, especially by the thickness of the walls.

Both Threave and Ravenscraig display gunloops of early pattern. These early gunloops are of either 'inverted keyhole' or of 'dumb-bell' form; also occasionally found are gunloops with cross-shaped openings. During the early part of the 16th century, however, a new form of gunloop was introduced and quickly became almost universally used in Scotland: that of the flattened oval, narrowing to a circle towards the back of the wall, through which the gun would project. The earliest appearance of this type is tentatively identified as being at the artillery blockhouse constructed at Dunbar Castle some time before 1523. This form was not widely adopted in England, where sill and lintel were also usually widely splayed. But within a very short period, this type was adopted all over Scotland (for example, of over 50 gunloops at Craignethan Castle, dating to c.1529-1540, all are of this type), almost totally replacing other forms of gunloop by its great practical advantages. Many examples – for example at Elcho Castle – show provision for a wooden bar at the inner end on which a gun could be rested, or the swivel pin of a gun located. In the latter case, the gun could be swivelled from side to side, and the horizontal oval shape came into its own. Some such gunloops were placed with the oval set diagonally, and not all run horizontally through the wall: most late-16th-century castles, if they were of L- or Z-plan, make some provision of cover for the main entrance, and such gunloops tend to be angled down from the upper storey, and it is very easy to work

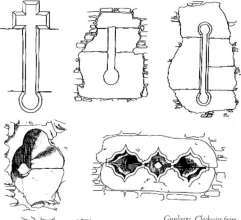

Gunloops. Clockwise from top left: crosslet, late 15thC; inverted keyhole, mid 15thC onwards; dumb-bell, mid 15thC onwards; decorative, late 16thC; oval mouthed, early 16thC onwards; decorative, mid 16thC

out, from the angle at which the opening goes through the wall, and the degree at which it is angled, just which weak spot in the castle's defences each particular gunloop was intended to cover.

This aspect is very readily apparent at Tolquhon Castle. What is even more notable about the Tolquhon gunloops, however, is their elaboration. Tolquhon, as has already been mentioned, was more than most castles making a pretence at defensiveness. But as well as the elaborate triple-gunloops, intended for display and not very effective, flanking the main route into the castle, the distribution of others — mostly of oval shape — has been very carefully considered.

But although so many of the later 16th-century castles are country houses built in the established military idiom, it had not been long since strongly defensible castles had been required — and were being built — throughout Scotland. Less than a generation separates the martial Noltland Castle, with its 71 gunloops, from Tolquhon. Noltland was begun some time after 1560, and Tolquhon dates from 1584-1589. And the number of castles heavily fortified against artillery during the early part of the 16th century — Craignethan of the 1520s and 1530s, Blackness (where the artillery fortifications were completed in 1543), even the strengthening of Tantallon following the siege of 1528 — stand in stark contrast to the state of affairs towards the end of the century.

The interesting aspect to Craignethan, Blackness and Tantallon, and, indeed, to the other early 16th century artillery fortifications such as Dunbar and the slightly later strengthening of Edinburgh Castle in the aftermath of the siege of 1573, is that all are in central Scotland, most of them in the Lothians.

Part of the threat during the early 16th century came from turbulent noble families, and part was as ever from England. For defence against Scotland's southern neighbour the defences of castles along the Firth of Forth were substantially upgraded. The military ambitions of Henry VIII were not confined to France, and conversely, the willingness of the French to play the Scottish card in their struggles with England, ensured that these defences were needed. Henry VIII's 'rough wooing '(the ironic name for the destructive English invasions of 1544 and 1545, following the Scots refusal to send the infant Queen Mary to England to be educated) was the culmination of struggles throughout the early 16th century: it is no coincidence that James IV was killed at the Battle of Flodden in 1513, and James V died sick at heart after hearing of his army's defeat at the Battle of Solway Moss in 1542.

THE CASTLE AT WAR

Castles were built, at least partly, to act as strongholds and it would be surprising if many of them had an entirely peaceful story to tell. For some, however, the strength of their position, the good judgment of their owners in always managing to be on the right side, the very fact that here was a fortified position (the castle had a deterrent value merely in its existence, often forgotten in modern expectation of battles and sieges), all might mean that a castle very rarely saw any testing of its defences.

Conditions varied, however, throughout the country and over the whole period. Between the 11th and 13th centuries, the Kings of Scots were gradually asserting their authority in the southwest (Galloway) and the north and northeast (Ross-shire and Moray), and the turbulent conditions and danger of open rebellion (which flared on a number of occasions) demanded defensive strongholds. But the heart of the kingdom was peaceful.

It was with Edward I's invasion and the ensuing wars, however, that things changed. In the 61 years from 1296, the fortunes of the Scots fluctuated, but no part of the country escaped involvement in the war. Only with the return of David II from English captivity in 1357 did Scotland regain a measure of peace with England. The rest of the Middle Ages presents, on the whole, a story of more limited border conflict with England and a gradual definition of the present border. Internally, the story is one of the Crown trying to assert its authority against powerful subjects and over the semi-autonomous Highlands and Islands.

Medieval siege techniques developed as castle defences developed and each was constantly being improved to try to circumvent the other. If the castle's garrison refused to surrender when called upon, or the initial assault failed, the attackers would settle down to besiege the castle, and to plan what might be done to hasten on the siege. The castle garrison, meanwhile, would be able to live off the stores it held and water from its well.

If the castle was well-prepared, and furnished with sufficient stores, it would be able to withstand siege for months (the first siege of Bothwell by the Scots, in 1298-9, lasted 14 months). If the garrison received due warning of a potential siege, they would ensure extra supplies, as when in 1306, the Scottish garrison at Kildrummy used the great hall to store extra grain, but were forced to surrender when this was set alight by a traitor and the resultant fire spread to the rest of the buildings.

The reason the siege of Bothwell lasted 14 months was that the Scots did not have the technologically sophisticated siege engines available to the English, so that the only alternative available to them was to sit down and starve the garrison into surrender. In a siege, the initiative tended to lie with the attacking force, and the garrison had to stay on the alert for sudden assaults and attempts to gain entry, either by trying to force the

Bothwell Castle, a reconstruction of the castle had it been completed as originally intended

main gate or by the use of specially built ladders. It was the defenders who tended to have a morale problem.

If they had the means, the attackers might try to pierce the walls. Mechanized warfare developed alongside the introduction of stone castles, both of them the legacy of crusaders' ventures to the Middle East. Although the principles behind the various sorts of siege engines, mangonels, trebuchets and ballistas (all of them stone- and missile-throwing machines) had been known since Classical times, they were not much used until the 13th century. They were effective in damaging the upper parts of stone walls and keeping defenders away from the parapets. At the same time, it was possible to try to breach the wall at its base, by using sappers or miners, as was done by the attacking Norsemen at Rothesay Castle in 1230. The battered plinths visible at the base of many castle walls, for example Skipness or the later work at Rothesay itself, were intended to make this as difficult as possible, and ditches and moats were designed to try to make it difficult to bring to bear mobile covers intended to protect sappers as they worked. These would be needed, as the activities of the sappers were extremely dangerous to the castle's defenders, and they would want to stop them. At some castles, notably at Hermitage and Threave, provision was even made for a timber bretasche or hoarding, a wooden galley with gaps in the floor, projecting out from the parapet, which made it easier to counter such methods. Over the years this was in some cases constructed in stone, as a so-called box machicolation (as can be seen, for example, above the entrance to the donjon at Bothwell Castle) and eventually around towers or along longer stretches of parapet, to give the typical corbelled silhouette of the wall-head of the towers at Caerlaverock or of the wall-head at Borthwick Castle. The identifying factor of machicolation is that there are holes between the corbels, coming down from the wall-walk, to allow missiles to be dropped on attackers.

As an alternative to breaking through the wall, attackers could try to dig underneath and undermine it. The mine, and

An example of machicolation

the counter-mine dug by the defenders to intercept it, together form one of the most fascinating features of St Andrews Castle. These were dug during the famous siege of 1546-7, and show how the attackers were on the point of widening their main tunnel to create as wide a gap as possible in the castle wall above when it collapsed. The timbers which would have been placed to support the roofs of the tunnels once they were beneath the castle wall would eventually have been burned and the wall brought down. In this case, because of the defenders' counter-mine, the mine was not completed. The castle was nonetheless captured, but by artillery bombardment.

A more usual method, however, of trying to capture a castle was to build a siege tower. This was a wheeled structure, tall enough that soldiers stationed on top could, once it was wheeled against the curtain wall of the castle, leap across on to the rampart and attempt to capture the castle. So, whereas the Scots laid siege to Bothwell for 14 months in 1298-9, presumably because they had no access to siege engines or towers, it took Edward I less than one month to recapture it in September 1301. Camped before the castle with an army of some 6800 men, Edward had a great tower, called 'Le Berefrey' or The Belfry, built at Glasgow. The prefabricated parts were brought to Bothwell and there assembled, and the structure was presum-

47

ably instrumental in the capture of the castle. Afterwards, it was carefully dismantled and carried in the train of the army.

Presumably a stone-throwing machine was the 'war-wolf' which five supervisors and fifty carpenters constructed for the siege of Stirling Castle in 1304. Whether it was the appearance of this on the scene or not, the garrison offered unconditional surrender before the machine had had a chance to see action, and King Edward, in high dudgeon, ordered that the surrender not be accepted nor the garrison allowed to leave before the war-wolf had been tried out against the walls of the castle.

Warfare during the rest of the middle ages was less momentous than the happenings of the Wars with England. Tower houses were not intended to be held against long drawn-out sieges. One Borders tower was captured by the English during a dawn raid by the device of hiding until the women came out in early morning to fetch water, and at that point forcing an entry – the most telling point here is that water had to be brought in from outside, making it plain that here was a tower which, however mild the attack, could not withstand a siege of more than a few days. In the Borders, raiding became endemic and a way of life on both sides: lairds made common cause with the ostensible enemy in order to raid other families on the same side of the border. Raiding meant driving off cattle and possibly burning a few crops and cottages, so most Borders towers would not have had to withstand a siege of more than a few hours. Unsettled conditions continued into the 17th century, leading to the widespread construction in the border counties of the fortified farmhouse termed 'bastles'

Just as turbulent were the conditions prevailing in the

Highlands. It was difficult to enforce the King's Peace in an area which contained remarkably few roads, and where royal authority was often in name only. As far as possible, the king used friendly clans to try to keep peace, hence the reliance upon the Campbells in Argyll. Nevertheless, feuds and clan warfare were common, and throughout the 17th century land holdings were fluid. Even in the Highlands the King's Peace eventually prevailed, but overseen by fortifications built, for example, by Oliver Cromwell and the Hanoverian government. These, however, belong to another story.

❈ ABERDOUR CASTLE ❈

ABERDOUR, FIFE

*A*lthough largely ruined, Aberdour's spectacular situation on the coast, overlooking the Firth of Forth and across to the island of Inchcolm, must be one of the most striking in Scotland.

HISTORY

The 13th-century tower house, built over an earlier structure, was strategically situated on the higher ground of the banks of the Dour Burn and commanded a fine outlook across the Firth of Forth. In the late 16th century the 4th Earl of Morton (one of the murderers of Mary, Queen of Scots' husband, Lord Darnley, and a notorious opportunist), modernized and upgraded the tower in keeping with his burgeoning status at Court. Unfortunately, Morton's meteoric rise (he became Chancellor in 1563 then Regent) was followed by an equally meteoric fall (he was executed in 1581). The 6th Earl of Morton continued the improvements to the castle but all the hard work and expense came to nothing when the 8th Earl loaned the property to a handful of officers from Queen Anne's army, under whose negligent occupation a considerable portion of Aberdour burnt to the ground. The last resident died in 1791, the castle was given over to pigs and cows and its stone plundered for building material. The state assumed responsibility for it in 1924.

FEATURES

The gaunt walls of Aberdour, rising against the backdrop of sea and sky, possess a haunting atmosphere all of their own. The

massive stone keep collapsed in 1844, destroying much of what remained after the fire and only a tiny part of this once great and splendid fortress remains intact. A painted wooden ceiling showing fruit, leaves, grotesques and the red heart emblem of the Douglas Earls of Morton has survived, however, and there is a spacious, well-lit gallery. The 4th Earl's ambitious plans for his castle included the creation of walled and terraced gardens and a bowling green (recently restored). The sundial is 17th century and there is a very large, beehive-shaped doocot (dovecot).

⚙ AYTON CASTLE ⚙

An imposing and distinctive red standstone castle, a *tour de force* of the Victorian Scots baronial revival.

HISTORY

The present castle at Ayton dates only from the mid 1840s, although the site is known to have been occupied since the early medieval period when the Norman de Vesci family lived in a small castle here. A later castle was besieged by the English in 1497 and, by the early 18th century, Ayton belonged to the powerful Borders family, the Homes. James Home was an ardent Stuart supporter, 'coming out' for the king in the 1715 Rising which, inevitably, led to the forfeiture of the estate to the Crown. In 1765 the Fordyce family acquired the property and in 1834 Ayton was burnt to the ground. In 1838 the site was sold to William Mitchell (later Mitchell-Innes in honour of his benefactor, the banker Gilbert Innes of Stow, near Lauder). Mitchell-Innes decided to build himself a fine new mansion more in keeping with his rising social status and, in 1845, commissioned James Gillespie Graham to draw up plans in the newly fashionable mock-Scots baronial style, complete with bartizans, crow-stepped gables and pepperpot turrets. Mitchell-Innes's son, Alexander, inherited the mansion on his father's death and extended it further to accommodate his large family (he was married twice). On Alexander's death in 1886 the estate was sold to Henry Liddell of Northumberland and the Liddell-Graingers still own and occupy Ayton.

FEATURES

Gillespie Graham's original internal plan for Ayton is simple: the main rooms lead off a ground floor corridor which runs the length of the house with, at either end, an additional wing to accommodate bedrooms and a service area; the later extensions were incorporated into this original scheme most successfully. Outstanding features at Ayton are the embossed plaster ceilings, woodwork and painted walls – the work in the corridor and hall is signed by the artists themselves. The fireplace in the dining room is worth a second glance: it is not, in fact, the original – this was bought from the owner by the American writer, Mark Twain, who clearly admired it greatly and persuaded the owner to take it out and sell it to him!

❊ BALGONIE CASTLE ❊

MILTON OF BALGONIE, FIFE

For over 600 years Balgonie's robust medieval tower has been clearly visible from far and near, and, even today, still dominates the countryside around with its commanding image of baronial might.

HISTORY

The name Balgonie is derived from a form of Gaelic which was used in Fife until around 1200, so it is likely that there was a much earlier settlement here, perhaps a hunting seat of the Earls of Fife. What we see today, however, was built by the Sibbald family and later bought by Field Marshal Sir Alexander Leslie in 1635. Leslie was the son of the Captain and Bailey of Blair Castle, important posts which suggest considerable prestige, and his son further enhanced the family's status by rising to become the Lord General of the Scottish Army of the Covenant. Leslie was created 1st Earl of Leven and his death, in 1661 at Balgonie, was marked by a midnight torchlight procession to the church of St Drostan, Markinch. The renegade Rob Roy occupied the castle in 1716 and by 1840 Balgonie was 'fast hastening to decay'. Now, however, the castle is very much lived-in and has become possibly the most romantic venue in Scotland for weddings!

FEATURES

The fine medieval tower forms the earliest part of the castle and, as is usual with such strongholds, has very thick walls (up to 11 feet), little windowspace and each floor sits squarely on top of the one below. The later range of buildings forms a hall house and was completed in 1496 (James IV visited Balgonie in August of that year and was so impressed by the masons' work that he gave them 18 shillings (80p), a colossal sum in those days). The impressive Great Hall of this part of the castle has two fireplaces, which were at one time 10 feet wide!

❈ BALLINDALLOCH ❈ CASTLE

BALLINDALLOCH, GRAMPIAN

Set on the banks of the River Avon, in the heart of the lovely Spey valley, Ballindalloch Castle is an outstanding example of 16th-century Scots baronial architecture.

HISTORY

The original builder of Ballindalloch initially intended to erect his castle on higher ground nearby but, as legend has it, as soon as night fell and his workmen left the site, an invisible force destroyed all that they had built during the day. At length the laird heard a voice directing him to build on the present site, which he did, and was probably wise to do so since his castle is still standing here, almost 500 years later! Perhaps more surprisingly, given the turbulent history of the clans, Ballindalloch has remained in family hands for its entire history — in spite of the fact that in the late 16th century the Grants of Ballindalloch vigorously pursued a bloody vendetta against their kinsmen, the Grants of Casson, which lasted for three generations! In the 18th century the castle was inherited by Ewen Macpherson, an active supporter of Bonnie Prince Charlie, who, after the disaster of the 1745 Rising, was forced to hide in a cave on his estate for nine years to evade capture. A reward of £1000, a colossal sum in those days, was offered for his betrayal by government forces but, although many of his tenants knew where he was hiding, the reward was never claimed. In 1780 the estate came into the hands of the colourful General James Grant who distinguished himself in the American War of Independence. The General added two wings to the castle, one of which was, reputedly, to house his French chef!

FEATURES

Ballindalloch is a typical Z-plan castle with two round towers placed at diagonally opposite corners. The design is standard mid- to late-16th century in style, although the precise date of construction is not known. Alterations over the centuries include a 17th-century caphouse added to the stair tower, a water tower and, after a fire in 1645, extensive rebuilding. General Grant's two wings were added in the 18th century, followed by a courtyard.

✹ BALMORAL CASTLE ✹

CRATHIE, GRAMPIAN

A cornucopia of mock-Scots baronial features, Balmoral is a perfect illustration of the mid-Victorian longing to recreate the 'romance' of the past.

HISTORY

Balmoral's story begins much earlier than 1852 when Queen Victoria's husband, Prince Albert, bought the estate for £31,000. It is possible that a 14th-century fortified manor existed on this site, but there was certainly a property here in 1484, since tax records for that year indicate a payment from 'Bouchmoral' (Gaelic, 'majestic dwelling'). The Gordons of Huntly owned the estate at that time and kept it until 1662 when it passed through various hands. In 1848 Queen Victoria, troubled by incessant rain and mist whilst on holiday at Ardverikie, visited Balmoral and was instantly attracted by the castle and its peaceful surroundings. After renting it for summer holidays for four years, the castle became royal property and Prince Albert, together with William Smith, the City Architect of Aberdeen, set about its recreation as a neo-Scots baronial mansion. Balmoral is still used by the royal family as a holiday retreat.

FEATURES

Mullioned windows, pepper-pot towers, balconies, crow-stepped gables, castellation and corbelling – all the typical Scots baronial features abound at Balmoral. There are two main

blocks of buildings, connected by wings, and the whole is dominated by a massive tower reaching to a height of 100 feet. The material is an attractive, light grey granite, quarried on the estate. The castle is designed to accommodate up to 100 people and the public rooms include a huge ballroom (approximately 70 feet by 25 feet), now housing an exhibition for visitors which includes paintings and other items from the Queen's private collection. This exhibition, together with the pretty gardens, is open to the public on summer weekdays; they are not open when the royal family is in residence.

❊ BALVENIE CASTLE ❊

First the stronghold of the powerful Comyn family, then of the wild and lawless Douglas clan, this sizeable 13th-century moated castle, now ruined, was once at the heart of the power struggles between clan and clan, and clan and king.

HISTORY

The substantial, if rather grim, remains of Balvenie reflect its historical significance as an important stronghold, firstly of the Comyn family, who guarded strategic communications routes through the hills, then of the unruly and rebellious Douglas clan. The present ruins date mainly from the Douglas occupation of the 15th and 16th centuries. The turbulent 'Black Douglas' earls caused considerable problems for the Stewart kings, one of whom, James II, took the somewhat extreme step of stabbing William, the 8th Earl, at Stirling Castle in 1452 (see Threave Castle). This prompted open rebellion against the king, but the Douglas clan suffered a decisive defeat in 1455. Their lands and property were subsequently forfeited to the Crown. The Stewart Earls of Atholl then took over the castle until the early 17th century (for an annual 'rent' of one red rose, payable on St John the Baptist's Day), and it subsequently passed through several hands, including the Innes and Forbes families. During the 17th century, Balvenie was frequently attacked by the marauding MacGregor clan and a group of Royalists were defeated here during the Civil War. In 1718 one William Duff committed suicide at the castle and Balvenie was abandoned as a residence. In 1928 the trustees made the castle over to the nation.

FEATURES

The remains of the 13th-century Comyn fortress lie beneath the more visible 15th- and 16th-century additions made by the castle's Douglas owners. These included substantially enlarging the property to form a courtyard castle, 150 feet by 130 feet, protected by a 25-foot-high, seven-foot-thick curtain wall, strengthened by towers. In the late 16th century a more stately mansion was constructed, by the fourth Earl of Atholl, within the enclosed courtyard, but damage to the stonework indicates that this was destroyed by fire. The round tower, with its attractive decorative details, dates from this period.

✺ BLACKNESS CASTLE ✺

Blackness, Lothian

Standing on its rocky promontory in the Firth of Forth, this little-known but well-preserved 15th-century military fortress has played an important role in the key events of Scottish history.

HISTORY

Blackness village was once an important port, acting as outlet for the royal burgh of Linlithgow and the castle was, therefore, of considerable strategic importance. Its exact date of construction is not known, but it was certainly burnt in the mid 15th century during the vicious clan wars, and restored and burnt again in the late 15th century by an English fleet. The castle's already strong fortifications were further strengthened by Sir James Hamilton of Finnart (see Craignethan Castle), who thickened the outside walls and made provision for cannon. The castle changed hands several times over the years and was besieged and damaged by Cromwell's forces under General Monck in 1654. Charles II had it repaired and restored and it was subsequently used as a state prison for distinguished Covenanters (those who opposed the king's religious policies). After the Act of Union in 1707 Blackness was one of the four key Scottish fortresses that were to be maintained and kept permanently at full military strength. In the 19th century Blackness was used as an ammunition depot and it became state property in 1912.

FEATURES

Blackness is often likened to a ship, because of its high enclosing walls and rather unusual shape. The tower, the oldest part of the castle, rises from the centre like a ship's mainmast. A careful restoration programme was undertaken by the state during which most of the 19th-century additions were removed and the upper sections of the tower taken back to their original appearance. There is a tradition that an underground passage runs from Blackness to the House of the Binns about a mile inland. A less fanciful feature of the castle is its grim pit prison, gloomy and miserable, its drain washed by the tide. Blackness has almost always been used as a fortress and therefore lacks any hint of the civilizing influence of domesticity; its striking situation, however, and its well-preserved, if austere, appearance have their own particular appeal.

❈ BLAIR CASTLE ❈

A vast, white baronial castle, much altered and extended over
the centuries since its earliest appearance as a 13th-century
tower.

HISTORY

When David Strathbogie, Earl of Atholl, returned from the
Crusades in the mid 13th century, he was considerably annoyed
to find that John Comyn, his neighbour, had not only trespassed
on Strathbogie land, but had even built himself a towerhouse!
The Earl complained forcefully to his king, Alexander III, his
rights were restored and the tower became Strathbogie property.
In the 15th century the Strathbogies forfeited both title and
estates to the Crown and both were later awarded to the Murray
family, the Earls of Tullibardine. Blair was damaged by
Cromwell's troops in 1652 and the 2nd Murray earl (who later
became a marquess) began to reconstruct and rebuild the castle.
The second marquess was made a duke by Queen Anne but, in
spite of this, family loyalties were seriously divided between the
two crowns, Stewart and Hanoverian. In 1746, George Murray,
younger brother of the duke and head of the Jacobite army, laid
siege to Blair, his own home (held by Hanoverian troops), giving
it the curious distinction of being the last castle in Britain ever to
be besieged. The castle sustained serious damage and subsequent
repairs and alterations swept away two storeys from the tower,
the turrets and crenellations and transformed Blair into an

elegant Georgian mansion. In the 19th century, however, tastes changed once again and David Bryce, the architect, was commissioned to 're-baronialize' Blair by restoring the tower's top storeys and adding towers, turrets and crenellations.

FEATURES

A treasure-chest of fine furniture, porcelain, paintings, costumes, tapestries and toys — Blair's 32 rooms, still sumptuously decorated in 18th-century style, offer a fascinating insight into Highland life from the 16th century to the present day. Of particular interest, however, is the Picture Staircase, a grand ceremonial staircase, its panelled walls hung with an array of family portraits, and an outstanding collection of arms and armour.

❈ BOTHWELL CASTLE ❈

BOTHWELL, STRATHCLYDE

𝑇his massive ruined stronghold is one of the largest and finest of Scotland's 13th-century castles.

HISTORY

Bothwell's strategic position — the nearby Bothwell Bridge over the River Clyde was for 300 years the only span across the river — inevitably meant that it was always a much-prized possession, particularly during the country's struggles for independence. Its massive walls and sheer size made it a hard-won trophy: Edward I, for example, in 1301 needed nearly 7000 fighting men, over 20 miners (to undermine the walls), a new bridge across the river, various siege machines and an assortment of carpenters, engineers and stonemasons. Faced with this onslaught the Scots surrendered after three weeks and for the next 30 years or so ownership seesawed between the Scots and English until, in 1337, Sir Andrew de Moray, Warden of Scotland, destroyed the building as part of King Robert the Bruce's 'scorched earth' policy against English aggression. A major rebuilding programme was begun by 'Archibald the Grim', Earl of Douglas and one of the notorious 'Black Douglas' family (see Threave Castle), and the castle later became the property of their cousins, the 'Red Douglas' family. Several changes of ownership then followed until Bothwell finally came into the hands of the Home family.

FEATURES

The 13th-century castle, built by the Norman de Moravia (Moray/Murray) family, was conceived on a massive scale and consisted of a great courtyard surrounded by a curtain wall. These walls are more than 15 feet thick in parts, rise to over 60 feet and are strengthened by round or square towers at the corners. The castle is dominated by a mighty tower with walls 15 feet thick and separated from the courtyard by a moat 25 feet wide and 15 feet deep. The tower rises to an astonishing 90 feet at its highest point.

⚜ BRAEMAR CASTLE ⚜

BRAEMAR, GRAMPIAN

Braemar Castle may be well supplied with towers, turrets and crenellations, but it is certainly no romantic Highland flight of fancy; indeed it owes its appearance to the much grimmer realities of politics and conflict.

HISTORY

Braemar was built in 1628 by John Erskine, Earl of Mar, who had a dual purpose in mind: to provide himself with a hunting lodge and to establish a base from which he could both defend himself from, and lead expeditions against, his enemies, the Farquharson clan. During the Jacobite Rising of 1688, the Farquharsons proved themselves to be the better fighters, and soon occupied Braemar on behalf of 'Bonnie Dundee'. The 'Black Colonel', John Farquharson of Inverey, decided to burn the castle to the ground to prevent it from falling into government hands. Ironically, having been destroyed by a John Farquharson Braemar was subsequently bought by a John Farquharson (in 1732), and, even more ironically, repaired and rebuilt by the government itself in 1748 (it was envisaged that Braemar would be a suitable army outpost to help control the Highlands). Thus Braemar was reconstructed purely for a military function, hence its present fort-like appearance. The Farquharsons of Invercauld regained the use of Braemar in 1832 and, in 1875, the castle became a family home.

The government reconstruction programme included rebuilding the outer defences, especially the unusual star-shaped curtain wall with its wide loopholes (more suitable for firing muskets than the earlier, narrower arrow-slits); installing the huge iron yett (gate); and heightening the tower. Inside, the rooms have low, barrel-vaulted ceilings and are designed to enable rapid movement up and down the stairs. The grim pit prison was in use until the early 19th century (when it was occupied by whisky smugglers). A rather more appealing reminder of Braemar's military occupation are the graffiti on walls and shutters, carved by bored and lonely Hanoverian soldiers.

❀ BRODICK CASTLE ❀

An imposing, yet welcoming, Victorian mansion, the island retreat of the affluent Dukes of Hamilton.

HISTORY

The lovely Isle of Arran has been much coveted for centuries and was, indeed, once occupied by the Norsemen, whose fortress is reputed to have stood on this site. However, the oldest part of the present castle dates back only to the 13th century, and there are extensions dating from the 17th century with a major remodelling carried out in the 19th century. Brodick was granted to James, Lord Hamilton, by James IV, together with the title Earl of Arran, and remained in Hamilton hands until 1958. The family acquired a fortune in the coal industry as well as, firstly, a marquessate and, subsequently, a dukedom. In 1843 the Duke married Princess Mary of Baden and in 1844 he commissioned the architect James Gillespie Graham to design a large extension in the then fashionable mock-Scots baronial style. The intention was to merge the old and new parts of the castle as unobtrusively as possible and this was, by and large, successfully achieved. The last private owner was the Duchess of Montrose and the castle was given into the care of the National Trust for Scotland in 1958.

FEATURES

James Gillespie Graham used matching red Arran sandstone for his 19th-century extensions and alterations and, at first sight, the

castle presents a harmonious whole. The 'join' with the older section is mainly visible on the south front and is particularly noticeable in the differences between the two sets of windows on the first floor. The architect also showed considerable restraint in his repetition of the original Scots baronial details, such as crenellation and corbelling, and the result, externally, is one of pleasing understatement. Internally the castle was decorated and furnished in the prevailing taste of the time and, today, filled with the Hamilton treasures and heirlooms, the rooms have a comfortable, easy, yet stylish atmosphere. The gardens are amongst the finest in the country and include woodland and Victorian gardens.

❈ BRODIE CASTLE ❈

Forres, Grampian

The 16th-century seat and family home of the Brodie family who have been associated with the area for over 800 years.

History

Unlike many Scottish clan families, the Brodies seem to have been neither particularly restless (they have been connected with the lands around Brodie Castle from at least the 11th century), nor particularly socially ambitious (they remain one of the oldest untitled families in the country). Nevertheless the Brodies have taken an active role in the key religious and political movements over the centuries. The 15th Thane of Brodie, for example, held strong Presbyterian convictions which caused the burning of his home in 1645 by Lord Gordon, supporter of Catholic Charles I and leader of Montrose's northern campaign. Some time later the Brodies found themselves supplying both camps in the 1745 Rising: the Hanoverian forces were willingly given provisions whilst Prince Charles's men helped themselves to whatever they found in the Brodie fields! The 18th and 19th centuries saw the Brodie fortunes vary, but the burden of debt always seems to have been present and even resulted in the estate's sale in 1774. Fortunately it was bought by the Earl of Fife, whose daughter was married to Brodie of Brodie and was thus 'kept in the family'! The estate is now in the care of the National Trust for Scotland.

FEATURES

The design of Brodie Castle is based on a typical 16th-century Z-plan layout with two towers and the usual defensive features such as crenellation, arrowslits and gunloops. The castle of 1567 was considerably altered in the 17th century and again in the 19th

century. The large, airy rooms in the eastern end date from this time and are the work of the architect William Burn. The ceiling in the diningroom, a positive riot of extravagant plasterwork, is well worth seeing. The Brodies' private collection of Dutch, Flemish and English paintings is on view, together with French furniture and English, Continental and Chinese porcelain.

❀ BROUGHTY CASTLE ❀

BROUGHTY FERRY, TAYSIDE

A well-restored 15th-century stronghold in a superb situation overlooking the River Tay.

HISTORY

The earliest part of the castle is its massive five-storeyed keep, constructed in the 15th century by Lord Gray who, in 1490, extended it into a true fortress. The castle's proximity to the ferry gave its owners considerable (and lucrative) control over this busy communications route, and they also levied tolls on ships using the Tay. The 4th Lord Gray is remembered in Scottish history as the supreme traitor, for it was he who, in 1547, after the English victory at the battle of Pinkie (near Musselburgh), agreed to surrender his castle to the English invaders. The 2000 troops remained in the castle until 1550 , when it was recaptured by the Scots with French help. Lord Gray escaped with his life, but forfeited his lands and property. Cromwell's army, under General Monck, captured the castle in 1651 and, by the beginning of the 18th century, Broughty was said to have 'ceased to be of any utility and, being neglected, fell into decay'. In 1855 the War Office bought the castle and restored it as a military stronghold, seeing it as part of the coastal defences programme prompted by the Crimean War. It was extensively enlarged internally and given a new gun battery.

FEATURES

The castle occupies an excellent defensive site on a rocky headland jutting out into the Firth of Tay, and was originally constructed as a crenellated tower house, surrounded by walls, themselves strengthened by three round towers. The castle is now a museum with exhibitions on Dundee's former whaling industry and the natural history of the Tay.

❈ BURLEIGH CASTLE ❈

MILNATHORT, TAYSIDE

The history of ruined Burleigh, once the proud seat of the Balfours, is a storybook tale of success, romance, betrayal, and, ultimately, loss.

HISTORY

Little remains of this once imposing castle, but it was clearly a building of some considerable size and importance. The Balfours, granted land by James II, began to build in the early 16th century, starting with the main tower. They were awarded a peerage in the early 17th century. The 5th Baron, however, through a combination of love, loyalty and foolhardiness, was instrumental in losing both title and lands. In 1707, the then Master of Burleigh fell in love with a servant girl and was instantly dispatched to the Continent to 'clear his mind'. Before leaving, he swore to his beloved that if she married before he returned he would kill her husband. The girl duly married and, on his return, the Master duly shot her husband dead. Burleigh fled but was caught and sentenced to beheading by axe. In the interval between sentence being passed and being carried out, however, Burleigh was spirited out of Edinburgh's Tolbooth Prison wearing his sister's clothes. He went into exile on the Continent but, always a loyal Jacobite, returned to support the Stuarts in the 1715 Rising, for which his lands and title were forfeited. The title was not restored to the Balfours until 1868.

Although much of it has been lost, the remains of Burleigh indicate that the early 16th-century tower formed the core of a quadrangular castle, protected by a curtain wall and a moat. All that remains today is the roofless rectangular main tower, part of one courtyard wall with an entrance and an unusual and rather eccentric smaller tower. This second tower is circular in the lower section but the upper section is corbelled out to form a square caphouse or watchroom; the tower is well supplied with shotholes. The date 1582 and the initials and arms of Sir James Balfour and his wife, Margaret, are carved on one gable and the red rose of the Balfours is visible on the other.

⚜ CAERLAVEROCK ⚜ CASTLE

CAERLAVEROCK, DUMFRIES & GALLOWAY

An extraordinary triangular castle, overlooking the estuary of the River Nith, and though ruined, said to be the finest medieval castle in Scotland.

HISTORY

Shield-shaped Caerlaverock, once surrounded by marshland, two wet moats and two sets of ramparts, was a formidable fortress indeed. The castle dates from the 1290s and was hardly complete when it was besieged by Edward I and held by the English until 1312, when Sir Eustace Maxwell, Keeper of the castle, declared for Robert the Bruce. Although it was instantly besieged again, Caerlaverock held out and, eventually, was partially dismantled by Bruce's men to prevent it from falling into enemy hands. In the 15th century Caerlaverock was rebuilt and strengthened and the gatehouse was converted into a tower-house. During the 16th century the castle changed hands several times, sustaining serious damage by the English around 1572. In the 1590s Lord Maxwell repaired the castle once again, adding wide gunports (for cannon) as a further defensive feature. His successor, the 1st Earl of Nithsdale, was responsible for the final alterations to the castle in the 1620s, the erection of an elegant Renaissance residential block, considered to be one of the finest examples of Renaissance architecture in Scotland. Lord Maxwell must have been heartbroken to see this beautiful building and,

indeed, most of Caerlaverock itself, besieged then torn down by the Covenanters just a few years later.

FEATURES

Visually one of the most stunning castles in the country, Caerlaverock's three mighty walls, equipped with gunloops and machicolations and strengthened by two huge circular towers and a twin-towered gatehouse, rise spectacularly from the wet moat. The triangular, shield-shaped plan of the castle is unique in Scotland and is particularly striking. Though much ruined internally, some fine carved stone panels have survived from the 17th century and, together with the tall windows and gracious fireplaces, indicate the atmosphere of elegant ease that characterized the 1st Earl's work, now, sadly, all but lost.

❊ CARDONESS CASTLE ❊

A late 15th-century tower house by the sea, seat of the wild and quarrelsome McCullochs.

HISTORY

Cardoness is named after the Anglo-Norman de Carines family who once held the lands here and, according to legend, perished completely by falling through the ice of a frozen loch whilst committing the unforgivable sin of merrily celebrating the birth of an heir on a Sunday! Be that as it may, the lands came into the hands of the McCullochs before 1450 and the castle is thought to have been built around this time. The McCullochs were a particularly wild and unruly family, constantly feuding with their neighbours and causing trouble. In 1622, through a mort-gage foreclosure, the McCulloch lands, including Cardoness, became the property of the Gordon family. The McCullochs resisted the transfer of the castle for several generations. In one particularly violent dispute in 1697 the McCulloch laird shot dead his Gordon rival, fled abroad but, on attempting to return, was arrested and sentenced to death. He has, however, achieved a kind of morbid notoriety by being the last felon to be executed on the 'Maiden', a Scottish version of the guillotine. Soon after, the castle was abandoned as a dwelling and fell into decay.

FEATURES

Cardoness stands in an elevated position commanding excellent views across Fleet Bay and on a site which, before the coastal road was laid, would have had good defensive advantages. Though much of the castle is ruined, the four-storey tower house is still impressive and notable for the first floor great hall, with its high windows, stone seats and late Gothic fireplace, equipped with decorated aumbry (recess) and saltbox. The two rooms on the second floor also have fine fireplaces and mural chambers with drains.

❈ CARNASSERIE CASTLE ❈

$\mathcal{A}$ fortified tower and adjacent hall house standing in a commanding position above the main Oban to Lochgilphead road, and an excellent illustration of late 16th-century domestic architecture.

HISTORY

Carnasserie was built by the Reformer, John Carswell, first Protestant Bishop of the Isles, Rector of Kilmartin and scholar, who published John Knox's Liturgy in Gaelic (1567) – thought to be the first book ever to have been printed in Scottish Gaelic. Carswell died in 1572 and the castle became the property of the Campbells of Auchinleck. Carnasserie was captured and partly demolished during the Monmouth Rebellion in 1685 when the Earl of Argyll blew it up.

FEATURES

Although Carnasserie appears to be a medieval tower house with a later hall house attached, both sections were constructed at the same time. The fortified tower house is of the usual design with a parapet walk for the lookout on top and plentiful gunloops and shotholes; the lower hall house has a corbelled turret. There are, however, some more unusual features at Carnasserie which mark it out from the ordinary and reveal the growing concern in this period to combine defensive features, such as turrets and gunloops, with decorative details and more emphasis on domestic comfort and convenience. The string courses, for instance,

which run round the walls are, in places, of very delicate craftsmanship and the corbelling is particularly well executed. The carved panels above the entrance door include the remnants of an inscription encouraging the reader to have faith in God. Internally, the tower follows the customary plan of vaulted ground floor cellars and kitchen, but there is a vast fireplace (fully big enough to roast an ox), bread oven, piped water system (using stone ducts) and a stone sink. The first floor is the great hall and the bedroom accommodation is above. Traces of a courtyard still survive with, above the gate, an arch with the initials of Sir Duncan Campbell and his wife, Lady Henrietta Lindsay, and the date, 1681 – just four years before the Campbells were forced to leave the castle to its fate.

✳ CARSLUITH CASTLE ✳

CREETOWN, DUMFRIES & GALLOWAY

A picturesque ruined tower house overlooking Wigtown Bay.

HISTORY

The lands at Carsluith were originally Cairns property but passed, in due course, to the Brouns (Brown), a prominent and prosperous family who also owned property near New (Sweetheart) Abbey. The last abbot of New Abbey was, in fact, Gilbert Broun of Carsluith (died 1612), a vehement opponent of the Reformation, a fact which probably contributed to the thoroughness with which the Reformers destroyed the abbey buildings. The strongly Catholic Brouns were also involved in a long-standing feud with the Protestant McCullochs of Barholm, which culminated in the murder in 1579 of McCulloch of Barholm by John Broun, who promptly fled, leaving his father to be fined the colossal sum of £40 for his son's failure to account for his deed. The Brouns emigrated to India in the mid-18th century, abandoning Carsluith which quickly fell into ruin. It is now in the care of the state.

FEATURES

The history of the castle's construction is not well documented, but it was evidently built in two stages. The first section to be completed was the rectangular tower house (now roofless), probably in the late 15th century. In the 16th century an adjoining wing was added, making the castle into an L-shape. Evidence of two separate stages of building can be seen in the corbelling,

for example, that on the north front being of an earlier design
than that on the east side. In addition, the projecting top storey
of the wing impinges on an old window recess and the rather
awkward emplacement of a window in this recess illustrates the
time-old difficulty of satisfactorily linking together a new extension to an existing structure. The walls are well equipped with
shotholes and gunloops and there is a panel over the entrance
door with the arms of the Broun family (a chevron with three
fleur-de-lis), the letter B and the date, 1568.

❈ CASTLE CAMPBELL ❈

DOLLAR, CENTRAL

*I*n a strictly hierarchical society the baronial castle was a potent symbol of power and control and there can have been few more awesome sights than that of Castle Campbell, its massive walls dominating not only the town of Dollar and the lovely Dollar Glen, but the hills and valleys for miles around.

HISTORY

Intriguingly first named Castle Gloom (it was situated in the parish of Dolour, between the Burn of Sorrow and the Burn of Care, and close to Gloom Hill), the castle passed to the Campbells of Argyll from the Stewarts through marriage in the 15th century. The present structure dates from the later years of that century and was probably built by Colin Campbell, a prominent political leader of his day, who was later rewarded for his services with an earldom and became the Earl of Argyll in 1457. It was Colin Campbell who changed the castle's name in 1489. The 4th Earl was probably the first Scottish noble to embrace Protestantism and the castle became a focus for the Covenanters (Protestants who opposed the king's religious policies). The prominent reformer, John Knox, is said to have preached at the castle. In 1645 Castle Campbell was besieged by supporters of the Royalist Duke of Montrose who failed to take it, although some eight years later Cromwell's forces occupied and then burnt it. The 8th Earl and 1st Marquess of Argyll paid the ultimate price for his family's beliefs and was executed as a traitor after the Restoration.

Features

The earliest surviving part of Castle Campbell is the massive 15th-century tower, 60 feet high. Structurally the tower is the most complete of the remaining buildings, the majority of which were added in the 16th and 17th centuries to bring the castle up to the standards expected of a family of the status of the Argylls. The sheer lack of space on the site, however, resulted in few fundamental changes. Castle Campbell can be reached by road to within a quarter of a mile or by a steep, but pleasant, climb through unspoilt Dollar Glen.

✖ CASTLE FRASER ✖

KEMNAY, GRAMPIAN

A magnificent expression of Scots baronial architecture at its most powerful and sophisticated.

HISTORY

Although there was a towerhouse already on the site in the late 16th century, when Michael Fraser decided to build his grand new house, it was clearly far too modest for his requirements. Fraser first constructed the great, square tower – still known as the Michael Tower – although the work was not completed until after his death when his son Andrew Fraser completed the transformation. Fortunately for posterity the castle was not damaged in the troubled 17th and 18th centuries, although the lands around were severely damaged. The Frasers themselves seem to have emerged relatively unscathed from these unsettled times, even collecting a Jacobite peerage from James, the 'Old Pretender', in 1723. The rich agricultural lands around the castle provided the family with a secure income and they were active in promoting the agricultural reforms which improved the quality of life for so many tenants on the large estates. This Fraser interest in 'improvement' did not, happily, extend to the exterior of their castle which, except for some minor alterations, remains much as it was when completed in 1636.

FEATURES

Castle Fraser is a typical 16th-century Z-plan design with two towers – one square (Michael Tower), the other a round or drum tower. It appears that Andrew Fraser, who continued the building work after his father's death, took the opportunity of embellishing his father's ideas in the process, and the finished castle is both larger and taller than originally planned. The corner turrets, for instance, are two storeys instead of one, the Michael Tower was heightened and there is a considerable quantity of external decoration, including the band of stone cannon. The great carved armorial frontispiece is an expression of power and confidence and is signed 'I. Bel', one of the two Master Masons (the other was Leiper) who worked on Castle Fraser. The interior of the castle was remodelled between 1814 and 1870, but most of this Victorian work has been removed.

⚜ CASTLE MENZIES ⚜

A spacious, 16th-century tower house illustrating the movement away from the grim, defensive keep to the more comfortable, open mansion.

HISTORY

This tall, stately castle stands guard over the routes to Loch Rannoch and Loch Tay and was, for many years, the clan seat of the Menzies family. The present castle was built by Sir James Menzies in the 1570s and replaced an earlier building burnt down by the Menzies' rivals, the Stewarts of Garth. However, as a shield over the doorway of the castle testifies, the Menzies and Stewarts were eventually united in marriage. The castle subsequently survived comparatively unharmed through the centuries, and with only relatively minor alterations and additions, until, in 1839-40, a huge west wing was added, designed by William Burns, and the interior was greatly altered. The last of the line died in 1918 and the castle changed hands several times until it was bought in 1957 by the Clan Menzies Society, which has undertaken restoration work.

FEATURES

Castle Menzies is a fine example of a 16th-century Z-plan tower house, with square towers at the north-east and south-west angles. The walls are plain but the eye is attracted upwards to the pleasing circular angle turrets and the crow-stepped gables. The ground floor is vaulted and the first floor contains the castle's principal public rooms with their attractive 17th century plaster ceilings. There is generous sleeping accommodation on the second floor, including a guest room where Bonnie Prince Charlie slept on his way to defeat at Culloden in 1746. The dormer windows on the attic floor are prettily decorated; an inscription on one reads 1577 IMB IN OUR TYME and, on the lintel of the window, PRYSIT BE GOD FOR EVER. The castle is spacious and well-lit and while it was given some defensive features such as gunloops, turrets and a single entrance guarded by a great iron yett (gate), these are balanced by a general atmosphere of comfort and openness coupled with a concern for aesthetic appeal.

❈ CASTLE SWEEN ❈

*P*robably the oldest stone castle on the Scottish mainland, Castle Sween has presided over lovely Loch Sween for over 700 years.

HISTORY

There are two schools of thought on the origins of the MacSweens who built the castle in the 12th century. Some aver that the MacSweens were descended from Sueno, Prince of Denmark, and it is known that the area was under Norse rule in around 1200. The other school of thought contends that MacSween is a corruption of the indigenous Gaelic name Suibhne. In any event the MacSweens were not destined to stay in the area very long for they supported the English during the Wars of Independence and, as a result, lost all their properties and titles in Scotland and removed to Ireland. In the early 14th century the Campbells acquired custody of Castle Sween from the Crown. In the 15th century it passed to the McNeills, whom the Crown made Constables of Sween; the McNeills retained the castle until it came to the MacMillans by marriage. Having survived relatively unscathed for 400 years, however, the castle was besieged and deliberately destroyed by the Royalists in 1647.

FEATURES

The design of Castle Sween is extremely simple and shows a strong Norman influence. It consists of four curtain walls (seven feet thick and rising to some 40 feet high), which were originally constructed without corner towers, although two were added

later. There are no holes or breaks in the walls, except for the main gate and a sea-gate, and they are notable for the large corner and flat (or pilaster) buttresses which give added support and are characteristic of Norman design. The main residential area, the tower, is, unusually, greater in area than in height and, as a result, appears to be rather squat. Though much ruined, considerable areas of the walls remain and the scale and proportions of this once-proud stronghold can readily be appreciated.

❈ CAWDOR CASTLE ❈

CAWDOR, HIGHLAND

*D*espite the aura of supernatural doom which surrounds its name, thanks to its appearance in Shakespeare's *Macbeth* (with which the present castle has no connection), Cawdor is, in fact, a much-loved, lived-in and well-preserved home.

HISTORY

The Thane of Cawdor, who was looking for a site to build his castle, was instructed in a dream to load a donkey with gold and, letting it go free, to follow it; where the donkey lay down, there should he build his castle. The Thane did as he was advised and the donkey duly lay down under a hawthorn tree – hence the preserved hawthorn tree in the basement of the castle keep which emerges through the floor and vanishes through the ceiling! Shortly after the Thane had built Cawdor, however, the heiress, the infant Muriel Calder, was kidnapped by Campbell of Inverliver and his six sons, on the instructions of the Earl of Argyll who dearly wanted Cawdor for himself. Muriel's uncles, somewhat belatedly, gave chase and, in the fighting that followed, Inverliver's sons all died – although he himself escaped with Muriel. In 1511 Muriel, aged 12, was married to the Earl of Argyll's son, John, and Cawdor came into the Campbell family in whose hands it remains today.

FEATURES

The core of the castle is a mid-15th-century tower house, subsequently surrounded by a court. Additional ranges of buildings have been added over the centuries, especially in the 17th century, but care has evidently been taken to coordinate newer buildings with those of earlier times and the result is one of pleasing harmony. The interiors reflect the tastes and interests of Cawdor's many Campbell

inhabitants and their varied possessions gathered over the centuries include tapestries, portraits and even the great iron gate or yett from the notorious Wolf of Badenoch's stronghold at Lochindorb. There are three distinctive gardens to enjoy and four nature trails.

⚹ CLAYPOTTS CASTLE ⚹

This distinctive Z-plan castle, now half-hidden in the suburbs of Dundee, has survived comparatively unscathed through 400 years of Scottish history.

HISTORY

The present tower house dates from the 16th century (the dates 1569 and 1588 are carved on the gables of the two towers), but there are records dating back to the 14th century which show the Claypotts lands as part of the demesne of the Abbey of Lindores. The builders of Claypotts Castle were the Strachans and, from the comparative comfort of the internal accommodation, it is evident that they intended it as a family home rather than, principally, a fortress. In 1601 the Strachans sold the castle and in 1619 it came into the hands of the Grahams of Claverhouse, one of whose scions was Viscount Dundee (also known as 'Bonnie Dundee' or 'Bloody Clavers'), the loyal and ruthless Stuart supporter who was killed at the battle of Killiecrankie in 1689. Claypotts was then forfeited and, in 1694, given to the Earls of Angus and Douglas in the hands of whose successors, the Earls of Home, it remains, though now in state care.

FEATURES

That Claypotts Castle should have survived so well is a remarkable achievement and, perhaps, demonstrates the good sense of its various owners in avoiding involvement in the major political and religious controversies of their day. The builders, the

Strachans, clearly did not anticipate major problems, for although the castle has some defensive features, such as the squared-off and corbelled watchrooms on top of the towers, the liberal supply of gunloops and the single small doorway, its internal arrangements reveal that its owners had domestic comfort and convenience very much in mind. The inside staircase, for example, runs continuously from the ground floor to the attic — an unusual feature in buildings  of this period which were usually constructed with the stair ending on the first floor and continuing upward from elsewhere on that floor, thus forcing any intruder to cross an open space. The main hall is open and spacious and there are as many as eight bedrooms in the towers.

✵ COMLONGAN CASTLE ✵

CLARENCEFIELD, DUMFRIES & GALLOWAY

A formidable 15th-century tower, its massive walls housing a honeycomb of rooms, closets and stairs.

HISTORY

Comlongan was constructed by the Murrays of Cockpool who became Earls of Annandale in the reign of James IV. The castle seems to have survived relatively unharmed from the various political struggles, national crises and wars of the last 500 years or so and has never been extensively altered, although a more recent mansion house now adjoins it. Comlongan has now been repaired and restored by its private owner who, at the time of writing, welcomes visitors and also offers accommodation.

FEATURES

Comlongan is a fine example of a substantial 15th-century tower house, built at a time when defensive considerations were paramount. The rectangular towerhouse (approximately 50 feet square) rises to five storeys (the walls are approximately 65 feet high), and is topped by a corbelled parapet. The walls are stark and unembellished and up to 13 feet thick in places; above the ground floor level these immensely thick walls are a warren of mural rooms, closets and stairs. Access to the castle was through a single entrance still protected by the original iron yett (gate). The only room within the walls of the ground floor is a miserable, unlit and unventilated prison; the great hall on the first floor has a stone-flagged floor, window seats, an attractive

fireplace, its lintel made of a single oak beam 12 inches thick and 10 inches deep, and a particularly fine aumbry (recess) decorated in late Gothic style. The rooms above are timber floored and each is equipped with fireplace and mural chamber with drain. The top storey at Comlongan, incorporating a crenellated parapet, has two small watchrooms with crow-stepped gables, connected by the open parapet walk. Each room is supplied with fireplace, drain and lamp recess – and must have warmed many a grateful lookout in the long, dark, winter nights!

⊗ CRAIGIEVAR CASTLE ⊗

ALFORD, GRAMPIAN

A fairytale tower hidden in the quiet, wooded hills of
Aberdeenshire.

HISTORY

The Craigievar Estate was bought from the hard-pressed
Mortimer family by William Forbes in 1610. Forbes, brother of
the Bishop of Aberdeen, had made his fortune from trade with
the Baltic ports and was known as 'Danzig Willie' and 'Willie
the Marchant of Aberdeen'. Danzig Willie completed the house
the Mortimers had begun in 1600 although he had little time to
enjoy it as he died shortly afterwards, in 1627. Forbes's son,
William, was created a Baronet of Nova Scotia by King Charles
but, in spite of this, raised forces for the Covenanters, those who
opposed the king's religious policies. The 4th Baronet, Sir
Arthur, remained firmly neutral in the 1745 Rising (thereby
ensuring that his castle would remain intact) but by the 19th
century Craigievar was in serious need of repair. Under the
direction of the City Architect of Aberdeen, John Smith, it was
restored, without significant alteration, to its original condition
and appearance. From this time until it passed into the hands of
the National Trust for Scotland in 1963, Craigievar remained
much as Danzig Willie had left it – even the installation of
water and electricity was achieved with the utmost discretion (a
bath, for instance, was concealed in an old servant's box bed!).

FEATURES

Craigievar is a seven-storey tower house, built on an L-plan, and is a fine illustration of the Scots baronial style at its most assured. The walls rise sheer from the ground and lean inwards almost imperceptibly until they burst forth into a froth of corbelled turrets, towers, conical roofs, balustrades and crow-stepped gables. The castle has only one entrance, defended by a massive outer door and an inner yett (iron gate). Inside, there are elaborately moulded ceilings and, in pride of place above the hall fireplace, a superb rendering of the Scottish Royal Arms, said to be the finest in the country.

❈ CRAIGMILLAR CASTLE ❈

DUDDINGSTON, EDINBURGH, LOTHIAN

A massive and dignified 17th-century ruin, closely associated
with the fateful life of Mary, Queen of Scots.

HISTORY

The barony of Craigmillar was acquired by the powerful and
wealthy Preston family in the mid-14th century; the central
tower dates from this time and the curtain walls were added
later. The Prestons were a family of some social standing and
their home a residence of quality and comfort. For nearly 300
years they played host to Scottish kings and queens anxious to
escape the hurly-burly of life at court in Edinburgh (just three
miles away). The most famous royal visitor was, of course,
Mary, Queen of Scots, who visited the castle so often that a
nearby hamlet, used to accommodate her retinue, was (and still
is today) known as Little France. In fact it was within the walls
of Craigmillar that the plot to kill Mary's second husband, Lord
Darnley, the 'young fool', was contrived. Although it is not
known whether Mary herself knew of the plot, she is thought to
have been in the castle at the time the plot was devised. In 1660
the Prestons sold the barony to the distinguished judge, Sir John
Gilmour, Lord President of the Court of Session, and
Craigmillar remained with his descendants until it was taken
into state care.

FEATURES

Despite the encroaching estates of modern houses Craigmillar remains an imposing and formidable castle, only partly ruined. The oldest section is the L-shaped tower, built around 1370, with the surrounding curtain walls completed the next century. These mighty walls are over 30 feet high with round towers at each corner and extensive machicolations. In the mid 16th century additional protection was given by a further walled enclosure and a moat. The range of buildings within the walls was extended in the 16th and 17th centuries. The Preston arms are still visible over the arched entrance and the lion rampant of Scotland stands guard on the battlements.

⚜ CRAIGNETHAN CASTLE ⚜

CROSSFORD, STRATHCLYDE

Chief stronghold of the wealthy and powerful Hamiltons, staunch supporters of Mary, Queen of Scots, this highly-fortified tower house was once one of the most important castles in Scotland.

HISTORY

The 16th-century tower house at Craignethan was constructed by Sir James Hamilton of Finnart, the illegitimate son of the Earl of Arran and an accomplished and artistic man who distinguished himself as the King's Master of Works – before turning to treason and ending his days under the executioner's sword. The Hamiltons suffered for their support of Mary, Queen of Scots, even going into exile for a time in 1579, after which the Hamilton properties were taken over and extensively damaged. In 1665 Ann, Duchess of Hamilton sold the partly ruined castle to the wealthy Hay family, and Andrew Hay undertook extensive rebuilding work as well as the construction of a new range, part of which is still occupied.

FEATURES

Strategically situated on a bluff overlooking the River Nethan, Craignethan is well served, on three sides, by natural defences, whilst the fourth side is protected by a deep ditch. Though ruined, the outer walls and towers are extremely well preserved and the oldest section, the tower house, is notable for its exceptionally ornate details. Perhaps the most interesting aspect of

Craignethan is the comparatively recent discovery of a caponier or tunnel in the deep ditch, possibly the earliest existing example in the whole of Britain. The installation of a caponier indicates that the emphasis on attack was moving away from the bombardment of the ramparts to the undermining of the vulnerable lower castle walls. The caponier, with gunloops guarding both sides of the moat, would provide defence against attack on the base of the tower house as well as subjecting the besiegers to a deadly barrage of fire.

❈ CRATHES CASTLE ❈

BANCHORY, GRAMPIAN

*I*t took almost 45 years to construct Crathes but it was time well taken, for this fine Scots baronial castle still stands intact, unscarred by history and unspoilt by its owners, the Burnetts, whose home it was for 350 years.

HISTORY

The Burnetts of Leys have held lands in this area since the time of King Robert the Bruce; an ivory hunting horn (still on show) was gifted to the family by the king as a symbol of their right of tenure in 1323. The castle itself was begun in 1553 and completed in 1596, although it is not clear why it took so long to build it. The Burnetts were clearly a practical, level-headed family, for they managed to avoid involvement in the uprisings and conflicts of the 17th and 18th centuries, thereby safeguarding their home and lands from destruction and despoilation.

FEATURES

Externally, Crathes is a typical, 16th-century tower house with the usual Scots baronial features, such as corbelled turrets, crow-stepped gables and conical roofs. Built in more unsettled times and with defence a priority, there is a single entrance guarded by a yett (iron gate) and the lower walls are windowless. Both externally and internally the Burnetts changed very little over the centuries and there are still items made for the original owners which help to create something of the atmosphere of a prosperous laird's house in the late 16th century. In particular there are the brilliantly painted bedroom ceilings which show allegorical and historical figures accompanied by verses, proverbs and exhortations addressed to the recumbent reader. During the 18th century a new wing was added and a further wing was built in the 19th century; this was destroyed by fire in 1966 and not rebuilt. The formal gardens are a composite of eight individual designs and date from the 18th century, as do the yew trees, masterpieces of the art of topiary.

☸ CRICHTON CASTLE ☸

CRICHTON, LOTHIAN

Rising majestically from the bare, rolling Lowland landscape, the great ruined castle of Crichton was once home of two of Scotland's most notorious and ambitious families, the Crichtons and the Bothwells.

HISTORY

The barony of Crichton was awarded to John de Crichton by Robert III in about 1370 and the tower house at the castle dates from this time. It was John's son, William, Chancellor of Scotland, who persuaded the young Douglas heirs to dine at Edinburgh Castle in 1440, an occasion later known as the Black Dinner, because the two young men were beheaded in front of the young James II (see Threave Castle). The 3rd Lord Crichton forfeited his lands to the Crown in 1483 because of his role in a conspiracy against James III, and the king then awarded the property to Sir John Ramsay, later Lord Bothwell. Bothwell also betrayed his king (by spying for England), so the Crichton lands were subsequently granted by James IV to Patrick Hepburn, later Earl of Bothwell. A successor, the 4th Earl, was third husband to Mary, Queen of Scots; he was found guilty of complicity in the murder of Lord Darnley, Mary's second husband and, in 1567, the Crichton lands were again forfeited to the Crown. Nine years later the title and property were bestowed on Francis Stewart, the wild, yet cultured, illegitimate grandson of James V, who became the 5th Earl. The 5th Earl's unruly behaviour finally proved to be intolerable and the

property was forfeited once again. Instructions given to raze Crichton to the ground fortunately were never carried out.

FEATURES

The 14th-century rectangular tower house was extended by a keep-gatehouse in the early 15th century and a further wing was added later. The final building work involved the creation of the north wing, later extensively altered inside by the 5th Earl and his wife, Margaret Douglas, in the late 16th century. Their most striking innovation was the elaborate courtyard, embellished with diamond-shaped stones in the Renaissance style and reminiscent of the Palazzo del Diamante at Ferrara. (Bothwell had been exiled in Italy and may have brought the architect with him.) By the time the 5th Earl was compelled to forfeit Crichton he had turned it into one of the most outstanding examples of 16th-century architecture in Scotland.

❈ CROOKSTON CASTLE ❈

CROOKSTON, GLASGOW, STRATHCLYDE

The tall tower of ruined Crookston, though now almost engulfed by the suburbs of Glasgow and Paisley, is a potent reminder of one of the most dramatic and romantic episodes of Scottish history – the reign of Mary, Queen of Scots.

HISTORY

Crookston stands on raised ground overlooking the White Cart river and was probably built in the 13th century over the remains of an earlier castle. In the 1330s the estate was passed to the Stewarts of Darnley (who later became the Earls of Lennox). Perhaps the best known of the family was Henry, Lord Darnley, who became the second husband of Mary, Queen of Scots. Legend has it that Lord Darnley actually proposed to Mary at Crookston but, in any event, the couple are known to have stayed here after their marriage in 1565. Mary believed her husband was the chief instigator of the murder of her favourite and confidant, Rizzio and, in 1567, Darnley was himself killed in a rather unlikely explosion which his wife was rumoured to have helped to plan. In 1572 Crookston passed to Darnley's younger brother and then changed hands several times until it was bought by Sir John Maxwell of Pollok whose family undertook essential repairs and finally presented it to the National Trust for Scotland in 1931. It is now cared for by the state.

FEATURES

Crookston is, principally, a tower house with very thick walls, strengthened by additional towers at each corner. It is unusual in that there is no defensive curtain wall and not as many gunloops as might be expected in a fortified tower house such as this, although the single doorway was very strongly defended with two doors and a portcullis. The wide outer ditch (about 12 feet deep) encircled by a raised mound (varying from two to 10 feet above the level of the surrounding ground) would have been a most effective defensive characteristic: as the castle is on raised ground the land slopes sharply away from the ditch (making access to it arduous), and the space between the top of the mound and the ditch would be filled with a formidable palisade (sharply pointed wooden stakes, planted very close together).

⚜ CULZEAN CASTLE ⚜

A romantic clifftop castle created by the great Robert Adam, and renowned for the sheer elegance of its Georgian interiors.

HISTORY

The site at Culzean has, for centuries, been associated with the Kennedy family, who suddenly gained considerable prominence through the marriage of James Kennedy to a daughter of Robert III in the 15th century. In addition, one of James's successors became a mistress of James IV, another fortunate liaison which was influential, no doubt, in bringing the title Earl of Cassillis into the family. When the 10th Earl inherited the medieval tower at Culzean in the late 18th century, he began to plan a complete remodelling of the old tower house and commissioned the leading architect of the day, Robert Adam, to draw up plans. The 12th Earl of Cassillis was created Marquess of Ailsa, taking the name of the isolated rock, Ailsa Craig, in the lower Firth of Clyde and clearly visible from the castle. The 5th Marquess of Ailsa gave the castle to the National Trust for Scotland in 1945 and Culzean Castle and Country Park is now the Trust's most visited property.

FEATURES

This beautifully proportioned building incorporates the medieval Kennedy tower house and, externally, belongs to the then fashionable neo-Gothic style. However Adam's innate good taste prevented some of the wilder excesses of other such revivals and Culzean is not overburdened by bartizans, battlements and turrets. Adam was, however, much happier working with the simple neo-classical Georgian style and Culzean is, probably, unsurpassed in Scotland for the elegance and harmony of its interior decoration, furnishing and design. The superb Oval Staircase, for instance, which was created to fill a bleak and sunless courtyard, and the circular Drawing Room, overlooking the Firth of Clyde, are masterpieces of Georgian restraint and refinement. During World War II Culzean contained the National Guest Flat, occupied by General Eisenhower, and an exhibition here traces his career and association with the castle. The Country Park extends to over 50 acres and has formal gardens, a Fountain Court, Swan Pond and Deer Park amongst other features.

✺ DARNAWAY CASTLE ✺

Forres, Grampian

*H*idden amongst the trees of Darnaway Forest and lying in the exceptionally beautiful Findhorn Valley, Darnaway Castle has, for almost five centuries, been the seat and home of the Earls of Moray.

HISTORY

Darnaway has been associated with the Earls of Moray since the time of Thomas Randolph, Regent during the minority of David II in the early 14th century. However the oldest part of the castle today is the banqueting hall, begun by Archibald Douglas, Earl of Moray, in about 1450 as part of his ambitious plans to erect a very grand edifice indeed. The Earl forfeited the castle to the king, James II, after the Douglas family fell from power (see Threave Castle) in 1455, but the king allowed it to be completed to the Earl's original high standards. The castle was a favourite of James IV, who gave it to his mistress, Lady Janet Kennedy, and Mary, Queen of Scots brought her court here in 1564. A completely new mansion was constructed round the remains of the old castle in 1810 for the Earl of Moray, and Darnaway is still a Moray property.

FEATURES

Alexander Laing's imposing Gothic mansion encloses the magnificent 90-foot by 35-foot banqueting hall, a rare and outstanding illustration of a 15th-century open timber roof; it is said to be one of the finest and most complete roofs of its kind still in existence.

❈ DIRLETON CASTLE ❈

DIRLETON, LOTHIAN

A picturesque ruin in what is said to be Scotland's prettiest village.

HISTORY

Three families were responsible for the creation of Dirleton and each of these very different families left their own mark, their own distinctive style on its fabric. The first of these families was the 13th-century Anglo-Norman de Vaux family who constructed a sturdily powerful, yet aesthetically pleasing tower house. In 1298 Dirleton was besieged by Edward I, as part of his plan to subdue the troublesome Scots; the castle held out for some time but, on the appearance of Edward's fearsome siege machines, was soon forced to come to terms. The terms were conciliatory: the castle would be surrendered but the inhabitants could keep their belongings and leave unharmed. In 1311 Dirleton was reclaimed by the Scots and severely damaged. Later that century the second of Dirleton's owners, the Halyburton family, came into possession. Their principal contribution to Dirleton was to enlarge and modernize the accommodation and strengthen the castle's defences. These innovations were, however, not quite acceptable to the third of Dirleton's owners, the powerful and influential Ruthvens, who acquired the property in 1515 and proceeded to build an up-to-the-minute Renaissance mansion house. The Ruthvens forfeited Dirleton to the Crown in 1600 after being implicated in a plot to kill King James VI.

The final siege came in 1650 when the castle held out only briefly against Cromwell's mighty cannon. This time the terms were not so conciliatory and three of the defending officers were summarily hanged from the castle's walls.

FEATURES

The de Vaux castle consisted of three towers, two round and one square, rising from the edges, and thus conforming to the shape, of the rocky platform on which they stood. The castle was protected by a deep moat, at least 50 feet wide; the entrance was approached across a movable wooden bridge and defended by two portcullis and two massive wooden doors. The Ruthvens' mansion rose a full three storeys and was enhanced by well-planned gardens and a bowling green, both of which are beautifully maintained to this day.

❈ DOUNE CASTLE ❈

DOUNE, CENTRAL

A military and domestic stronghold of considerable strategic importance as well as a popular hunting palace and royal residence, Doune is, today, one of Scotland's largest and most sensitively restored late medieval castles.

HISTORY

Doune was constructed in the late 14th century by Robert Stewart, Duke of Albany, Regent of Scotland and an ambitious politician who possibly aspired to the throne of Scotland for his own branch of the Stewart family. It was while under Albany's 'care' that the young heir to the throne, the Duke of Rothesay, died in mysterious circumstances. In 1425 the Duke's son and successor as Regent, Murdoch, was executed by order of King James I, who confiscated Doune and it was to be many years before the Stewarts regained their castle, first as custodians, later as lords (1570). Although the castle suffered little physical damage in the turbulent 16th and 17th centuries, Doune was taken by Bonnie Prince Charlie's followers in 1745-6 and used as a prison. Escape from such a formidable and strongly-guarded fortress might, perhaps, be thought impossible but, so it is said, one prisoner did manage to escape from the Retainer's Tower – by the simple and time-honoured means of climbing down a rope of knotted cloth!

FEATURES

Strategically situated by the
River Teith and Ardoch Burn
and using these as natural
moats, Doune is guarded on its
third side by a man-made moat
and steep earthworks. The
Teith flows into the Firth of
Forth from the Highlands and
thus formed a major highway
from Edinburgh to the north.
The fortress of Doune, therefore, was perfectly placed to
guard and control communications along this route. The
most interesting feature of the

castle is undoubtedly the gatehouse complex: the formidable
gatehouse tower itself, fully 95 feet at its highest point, has
immense walls, a massive nine feet thick. The impressive Lord's
Hall and efficiently planned kitchens illustrate Doune's role as a
Stewart residence; the vast royal banquets, for example, would
be supervised and controlled by the steward from his special
room, cut into the thickness of the wall overlooking the hall.

❈ DRUM CASTLE ❈

DRUMOAK, BY BANCHORY, GRAMPIAN

Drum Castle is an intriguing architectural illustration of the changing tastes and fortunes of a single family, the Irvines, who made their home here for over 650 years.

HISTORY

When King Robert the Bruce granted lands along the Dee to his armour bearer and chief clerk, William de Irwin (Irvine) of Dumfriesshire in 1323, the new owner, on arrival at his estate, found a substantial square tower house already in place. Eight generations of Irvines subsequently occupied the tower, gradually becoming well-established in the area and methodically building up the family fortunes. Alexander, the 9th laird, was so wealthy, in fact, that he was apparently in a position to lend money to the King, James VI! In any event he decided to build himself a grand new house alongside the old tower house. Alexander's initials, and those of his wife, Margaret Douglas, are still visible, carved over one of the dormer windows. The date, however, reads 6191 instead of 1619 and was, perhaps, carved by an inattentive (and probably illiterate) mason at the end of a long day. Ten years later, however, the Irvines were caught up in the troubled political situation and their fine new mansion was attacked and ransacked. The family fortunes then sank so low that the laird felt unable to accept King Charles II's offer of a title, the Earl of Aberdeen. However, more settled times returned and the 18th and 19th centuries saw the Irvines prosper once again.

FEATURES

The great, plain tower which dominates Drum is a fine example of a Scots tower house, standing 70 feet high and with walls up to 12 feet thick. The 9th laird's 17th-century mansion was linked to the main tower and this later design, horizontal rather than vertical, indicates that the supply of structural timber was plentiful – possibly due to the expansion of trade between Aberdeen and the Baltic ports. Alterations made in the 19th century imposed more ordered and elegant internal arrangements and the Victorian extensions and remodelling included the restoration of the immense vaulted hall.

❊ DRUMLANRIG CASTLE ❊

Thornhill, Dumfries & Galloway

A splendid pink sandstone palace, housing one of the finest private art collections in the country.

History

The Douglas family had lived in a, by comparison, fairly modest castle here for some 300 years when William, 1st Duke of Queensberry, decided to build himself a grand new 17th-century mansion befitting his elevation to the dukedom. The castle took many years to build and almost ruined the family; in fact the duke, having completed it and, presumably, been presented with the final accounts, was so shocked at the cost that he spent only one night here, fleeing in horror to his property at Sanquhar. In 1810 Drumlanrig became the property of the Dukes of Buccleuch, who still own it.

Features

Drumlanrig is, architecturally, a kind of hybrid: it exhibits some of the traditional features of a Scottish fortified castle (it follows the quadrangular-courtyard castle design, for example, the corners strengthened by towers topped with corbelled bartizans, together with the characteristics of the grand stately home of a later age (the numerous large, pedimented windows reaching right down to ground floor level and the ornate arched and colonnaded entrance, for instance). The public rooms are richly decorated with fine carving (including some by Grinling Gibbons) and plaster ceilings, which often feature the Douglas

crest, a winged heart surmounted by a crown. The art collection comprises fine furniture (including two Louis XIV cabinets), tapestries, silver, paintings and family portraits by Rembrandt, Leonardo da Vinci, Holbein, Murillo, Ruysdael, Reynolds and Ramsay. The sumptuous elegance of Drumlanrig may perhaps belie the fact that it was built in what was still, in many ways, a dangerous age – a timely reminder of which is the room in which Bonnie Prince Charlie slept for one night on his hurried retreat from defeat at the battle of Derby (1745).

❈ DUART CASTLE ❈

*P*roudly standing guard over the beautiful Sound of Mull, this island stronghold was, for centuries, the seat of the Chiefs of the Clan Maclean. It was reacquired by them in 1911.

HISTORY

The Macleans of Duart trace their lineage back to a 13th-century ancestor, Gillean of the Battle Axe, and their castle was built by one of his heirs, Lachlan Lubanach Maclean of Duart. The power struggles between clans and, indeed, within the clans themselves, meant that a chief's stronghold had to be especially strongly fortified to withstand sudden, and violent, onslaught. Duart certainly fulfils this criterion, with its vast curtain wall and massive tower. For many years the Macleans supported the rightful Lords of the Isles, to whom they owed first allegiance, against both the Scottish and English rulers, and only after the last undisputed Macdonald claimant to the Lordship of the Isles died (in 1545), did they, slowly, submit to the Scottish crown. Always fiercely proud and independent, however, the Macleans continued their unruly and lawless ways until, in the early 17th century, Hector Og Maclean, together with other island chiefs, was forced to agree terms with the king, which included the destruction of all his galleys and the prohibition of all guns, cannons and double-edged swords. The Macleans remained loyal to the Stewart Royal line throughout the 17th and 18th centuries, although Duart was burnt by the Duke of Argyll and forfeited after the battle of Culloden (1746), after which it fell into ruin.

The castle was repurchased in 1911 and restored by the then Clan Chief, Sir Fitzroy Maclean, and is now the worldwide clan centre and home of the Chief.

FEATURES

Duart stands high on a rocky outcrop above Duart Point, a position which offers both excellent natural protection from attack as well as panoramic views. The massive curtain walls, almost 10 feet thick and 30 feet high, date back to the 13th century and surround two sides of the courtyard, the third, seaward side of which is bounded by the huge 14th-century tower house. A deep ditch was cut in the rock beyond the wall to give added protection. Later additions and alterations were made in the 16th and 17th centuries and Duart was restored in 1911-12.

❀ DUFFUS CASTLE ❀

DUFFUS, GRAMPIAN

*R*ising boldly and dramatically from the flat fields around it, ruined Duffus is a fascinating reminder of the relentless sweep of Norman ambition.

HISTORY

During the 12th century the increasing influence of the Normans began to be felt in Scotland, with the active encouragement of Scots kings from David I onwards. The Normans built strongholds, utilizing any naturally strong site, preferably with some height, which they would increase artificially if necessary. Here they would construct a simple motte and bailey castle, surrounded by palisades and a ditch, and with the owner's wooden residence on top of the mound. Although the wooden buildings and palisades have, of course, long gone, Duffus is still regarded as a superb example of a motte and bailey structure; its original wide, circular ditch is still visible and the artificial mound still rises dramatically and unexpectedly from the flat landscape. Duffus was built in the 1140s by the Norman de Moravia (Murray) family, and passed, by marriage, to Sir Reginald le Chen (Cheyne). He replaced the wooden buildings with a more substantial stone castle with a striking 14th-century tower which rose a full three storeys from the top of the old Norman motte, and must have been visible for many miles around. In the latter half of the 14th century Duffus changed hands once again through marriage and became the property of the Sutherland family who retained the title of

Lord Duffus. Duffus was sacked and partly destroyed by the unruly Douglas clan in 1452, but was rebuilt with additions. It was abandoned in 1705.

FEATURES

Duffus was evidently a strong and substantial structure extending, in total, over an area of around 8 acres. Although much ruined, the remains of the tower and the curtain wall give an indication of the castle's size and strength. Unfortunately, after 800 years, the motte is proving to be unequal to the task of supporting the weight of the tower and part of it has begun to slide down the slope.

✷ DUMBARTON CASTLE ✷

DUMBARTON, STRATHCLYDE

$\mathcal{T}$his strange, isolated rock in the River Clyde has been used as a fortress from at least the 5th century until 1945.

HISTORY

The Ancient Britons were the first to recognize the excellent strategic and defensive potential of the 254-foot-high basalt rock that later became known as Dun Breatann, the 'fortress of the Britons'. By the late 13th century the fortress had become a royal stronghold, much coveted by both the English and the Scottish kings, and, like many other castles, played its part in the turbulent events that characterized the reign of Mary, Queen of Scots. After the Scots' defeat at the Battle of Pinkie in 1547, Mary (aged five) was housed at Dumbarton for some weeks before being taken to France, escorted by a French fleet. The castle was then occupied alternately by Scottish and English forces but was regained for Mary after her return to Scotland in 1561. In 1571 Mary's reign was over and she had fled to England, to throw herself on the dubious mercies of Queen Elizabeth I, but Dumbarton still held out for her. However, a supremely daring attack by Thomas Crawford of Jordanhill who, by using only 100 men and scaling the least accessible face of the rock at night, achieved total surprise and the garrison surrendered. So complete was the surprise, in fact, that none of Crawford's men was killed and only four of the defenders. Later the castle became a prison, then barracks, but was abandoned as obsolete in 1865. Its active life was not yet quite over, however, for it was recommissioned by the army in the First World War and was also in use in the Second World War. It is now in the care of the state.

FEATURES

Dumbarton was never intended to be a family residence, it is simply a functional building and, as such, has none of the charm or aesthetic appeal of a home. In addition its several centuries of battle and bombardment mean that there is little left of its early structure, and most of what we see today are the fortifications which date from the 17th and 18th centuries. More interesting reminders of its past, perhaps, include the sundial, gifted by Mary, Queen of Scots, and a rather crude carving of Sir John Menteith, betrayer of the Scots patriot, William Wallace, in 1305; Sir John is depicted with his finger in his cheek, the traditional sign of betrayal. There are superb views up and down the River Clyde from the White Tower.

DUNBAR CASTLE

Dunbar, Lothian

The fragmentary ruins of a once-formidable stronghold, whose long history is tinged with romance and tragedy.

History

Standing on a windswept promontory overlooking the harbour of Dunbar, the ruins of this fortress can only hint at the castle's original size and strength. The earliest buildings appear to date from the 12th century and form a courtyard castle, well fortified and protected. Besieged in 1339 by the Earls of Arundel and Salisbury, the castle was successfully defended for six weeks by 'Black Agnes', Countess of Douglas and daughter of the Earl of Moray, until relief supplies arrived by sea. Over two centuries later, another notable Scotswoman would find herself in danger within Dunbar's walls, but this time her enemies were more subtle and duplicitous. The woman was Mary, Queen of Scots, and it was to Dunbar that Mary fled, with her second husband, Lord Darnley, to escape the furore at Holyrood following the murder of her secretary and confidant, Rizzio. The following year, after the explosion that killed Darnley, Mary spent 10 days at Dunbar with Lord Bothwell, who she had made keeper of the castle, and was soon to make her third husband. And it was from Dunbar that Mary and Bothwell gathered their supporters and set out together, for the last time, to fight at the battle of Carberry Hill in June 1567. After Mary's disastrous defeat, Bothwell returned alone, briefly, to Dunbar before beginning the final phase of his life as a fugitive and exile. In revenge, perhaps,

for its role in these events as well as because of its strategic
importance and considerable strength, Dunbar was dismantled
by Regent Moray in 1567 on the orders of Parliament.
Dunbar's final indignity was perpetrated by Cromwell's forces
who, after the battle of Dunbar in 1650, ordered stones from
the castle to be used to improve the town's harbour.

FEATURES

Although little remains of Dunbar's mighty, red sandstone
fortress, fragments and foundations still cling tenaciously to
their picturesque, rocky headland and, for those with an affinity
for Scottish history, make their own haunting commentary on
the tragedies of the past.

⚜ DUNDONALD CASTLE ⚜

DUNDONALD, STRATHCLYDE

A striking hilltop ruin, once a favoured royal residence of the first Stewart monarchs.

HISTORY

An earlier castle on this site, thought to have been a 13th-century tower house, was the home of the powerful Fitzalan family, supporters of King Robert the Bruce. The close association between the two families was further cemented by the marriage of Bruce's daughter to a Fitzalan son, and the eldest son of this union became Robert II, the first of the Stewart kings of Scotland. As the earlier structure had been largely destroyed during the Wars of Independence, Robert II rebuilt the castle as a large and impressive tower house and Dundonald became a much-favoured royal residence of both Robert II and his son, Robert III. After Robert III's death at Dundonald in 1406, the castle seems to have become rather neglected, its decay hastened by the 1st Earl of Dundonald, who removed much of its fabric in the mid-17th century to build a mansion nearby.

FEATURES

Dundonald's position, on a lonely, isolated hill overlooking wide, level countryside, is possibly its most impressive feature. The structure of Robert II's castle follows the usual 14th-century tower house pattern, but is on a larger and more elaborate scale, as befits its royal status. There are two lofty, barrel-vaulted additions to the tower house, itself an adaptation and

modernization of the older keep-gatehouse. The great hall was on the third floor and measured over 60 feet long by almost 25 feet wide. Its gracious proportions were augmented by an impressive vaulted ceiling, the ribs of which, though purely decorative, spring from elaborately moulded corbels on the side walls. The castle, now in the care of the state, has recently undergone extensive repairs.

✶ DUNNOTTAR CASTLE ✶

Stonehaven, Grampian

A grim, ruined fortress spectacularly situated on an isolated rock, high above the sea.

HISTORY

Although there have been buildings here since, possibly, the 9th century, the present castle was constructed by Sir William Keith, Great Marischal of Scotland, who erected a tower on the rock in the 1390s. The Marischal summarily destroyed a small chapel on the rock in order to build his tower, for which action he was promptly excommunicated by the Bishop of St Andrews, but pardoned by 'recompense' on the orders of the Pope. The Marischal's successors, recognizing the almost unassailable position of the rock, continued his building programme, fortifying and enlarging Dunnottar until it became almost a small community in itself. In 1651 Dunnottar, the last uncaptured fortress, was besieged by Cromwell's army and proved unbreachable by force, in spite of fierce bombardment. Starvation, however, compelled the defenders to surrender after eight months, although the Parliamentarians failed to find what they wanted; Charles II's private papers and the Scottish regalia had long been bravely smuggled out by Anne Lindsay. Perhaps the blackest point in Dunnottar's history came in 1685 when 122 men and 45 women, Covenanters who opposed the king's religious policies, were crammed into a small dungeon for two months during the summer. Nine of them died in the unspeakable conditions, which included torture. In 1716 the castle was destroyed by the

Duke of Argyll (the 10th Earl Marischal having sided with the Jacobites in the 1715 Rising) and it was dismantled in 1718, the year it was formally forfeited.

FEATURES

The oldest surviving building is the L-shaped, four-storey keep, still reaching almost to its full height of 50 feet, which dominated and controlled the entry to Dunnottar. The keep (1392) was later strengthened by a massive gatehouse (1575). In the 16th and 17th centuries four ranges of domestic buildings (including large kitchens, bakery and brewery) were added, and these, together with the great well which stretches 30 feet across, indicate that Dunnottar supported a fairly substantial number of occupants and was almost, in fact, a fortified township.

DUNROBIN CASTLE

GOLSPIE, HIGHLAND

Dunrobin deals in superlatives: it is one of the oldest continuously inhabited Scottish castles and the seat of the Earls of Sutherland, said to be the most ancient of the Earls of Scotland; moreover it is the most northerly of Britain's grand houses and certainly its French chateau-inspired design must make it one of the most unusual and, with 189 rooms, one of the largest!

HISTORY

The history of the Sutherlands is a complex and tangled one, and began in the 12th century when William the Lion granted lands in Sutherland to Hugh Freskin; the earldom was created later, in 1235. From the late 15th century, however, the earldom was the subject of a 'takeover bid' by the Gordon family, who used the usual methods of the time, such as making charges of idiocy and illegitimacy, coercion, marriage and, even, murder. Nevertheless the Sutherlands continued quietly and doggedly amassing great wealth and power until the heiress, Countess Elizabeth, married the Duke of Stafford in 1785. This marriage, to a man described at his funeral as 'the richest man who ever died', took the Sutherlands into the realms of unimaginable riches and made them the wealthiest landowners in the country and, possibly, in Europe. It was Countess Elizabeth, however, whom history (and long Highland memories) remember as the instigator of the notorious Highland Clearances, when hundreds of tenant farmers were forcibly evicted to make way for Lowland sheepfarmers. A dukedom was bestowed on the Sutherlands early in the 19th century and it was the 2nd Duke who commissioned the architect, Sir Charles Barry, to enlarge and remodel Dunrobin in the French style between 1845 and 1851.

FEATURES

Standing on a natural terrace overlooking the sea, Dunrobin today is largely Barry's creation and is a mixture of styles in which, for example, elegant neo-French towers co-habit with neo-Scots baronial crow-stepped gables. A fire in 1915 resulted in further reconstruction, by Sir Robert Lorimer; his panelled library and diningroom are particularly pleasing. A fine collection of tapestries and paintings by Canaletto are well displayed in Lorimer's drawingroom. The gardens are a delight.

❊ DUNSTAFFNAGE ❊ CASTLE

A once-mighty Campbell stronghold guarding the beautiful
Sound of Mull and Firth of Lorne.

HISTORY

This strange, dark fortress, standing on an isolated plug of rock
on a promontory in the Firth of Lorne, was built in the 13th
century by the mighty Ewen MacDougall, Lord of Lorne. The
Lords of Lorne did not enjoy their new seat for long, however,
for they chose to fight against Robert the Bruce and, in 1308,
lost their titles and properties. Bruce, recognizing the castle's
strategic value, made it a royal castle and placed it under the care
of the Campbell Earl of Argyll. In the 15th century the castle
was given by the earl to a Campbell kinsman and was held by
the Campbells, as hereditary captains, from then on. At this time
the Campbells were loyal Stuart supporters and were frequently
involved in expeditions and forays throughout the western
region, their castle acting as a focus of Stuart support. In 1689,
however, they changed their allegiance; Archibald, the 9th Earl,
opposed Catholic James VII and gathered his forces against the
king from Dunstaffnage. As a result the castle was partly
destroyed by James's troops but the family regained their power
and influence under a grateful William III. From then on the
Campbells always remained loyal to the London-based government of the day, refusing to help the Stuarts in either the 1715
or 1745 Risings. In fact, they even allowed Dunstaffnage to be

used as a temporary prison for Flora Macdonald, the woman who helped Bonnie Prince Charlie escape to Skye after his disastrous defeat at Culloden in 1746.

FEATURES

The 13th-century wall enclosing the castle stands over 60 feet high and is almost 10 feet thick; its contours follow the irregular shape of the rock on which it stands, thus giving the castle maximum security from attack. These massive walls were further strengthened by three round towers, augmented in the 16th century by a gatehouse tower which was accidentally burnt down in 1810. The castle is now in the care of the state.

✸ DUNVEGAN CASTLE ✸

ISLE OF SKYE, HIGHLAND

*T*his massive pile, originally accessible only by sea, has for centuries been the seat of the Chiefs of Clan MacLeod, strong and impregnable, yet touched by the very essence of Highland myth and romance.

HISTORY

The story of Dunvegan begins with the wall of enclosure built in the 13th century round the rock on which the castle now stands, by Leod, son of Olaf the King of Man and the Northern Isles. Over the centuries the MacLeods extended and consolidated their power from this remote fastness, taking a full part in the bloody clan wars of the 15th century and, from time to time, in the equally bloody internecine struggles for the position of Clan Chief. By the 17th century, however, the MacLeods had accepted the authority of the king and, indeed, become staunch Royalists, to the extent of losing some 700 clansmen on behalf of Charles II at the battle of Worcester in 1651. This terrible loss decimated their numbers and they did not take any important role in the 1715 and 1745 Risings. Support for their impoverished clansmen in the famine years of the 19th century contributed to the family's bankruptcy and the castle was let for several years. Happily it is now once again the seat (and home) of the Clan Chiefs.

FEATURES

Seven hundred years of alterations and extensions mean that Dunvegan is something of a hotch-potch of building styles. Nevertheless its brooding strength is certainly impressive and the interior, filled with the accumulated treasures, trophies and keepsakes of the centuries, is a delight. The Fairy Flag, for example, supposedly given to the 4th Chief in the 14th century by a fairy, is, though threadbare and torn, held in the greatest esteem; its presence at a battle guaranteed a MacLeod victory and World War II airmen even wore replicas of it under their jackets! (According to legend, however, the protective powers of the Flag can be used only once more.) Rather more prosaically, perhaps, the grim bottle-dungeon reminds visitors of the less appealing aspects of the history of this ancient clan centre.

⚜ EDINBURGH CASTLE ⚜

EDINBURGH, LOTHIAN

*F*ortress, palace, treasury, royal residence, refuge, prison and place of execution – the story of Edinburgh Castle is the story of Scotland itself.

HISTORY

Standing tall and proud on its volcanic rock, 443 feet high, Edinburgh Castle dominates the sprawling city that has grown up around it. Much battered, besieged, repaired, rebuilt and extended over the past 900 years (the earliest building still extant is the tiny 11th-century St Margaret's Chapel, built in honour of Malcom III's wife), Edinburgh soon became the focus of Scottish national feeling and loyalty. Because of this it was seen as a crucial prize to be won by those struggling for power, particularly in the wars between England and Scotland. Edward I, for example, besieged the castle in 1291; it surrendered after eight days and became an English garrison until 1313, when it was taken in a surprise attack by the Earl of Moray. Robert the Bruce ordered the castle and defences to be destroyed (except St Margaret's Chapel), although what was left was soon once again under English control. Another daring Scots' victory came in 1341 when William Douglas and his friends, disguised as merchants, dropped their cartloads of corn and wine between the open gates, then rushed in and captured the castle. David II subsequently returned to Scotland from imprisonment in England, assumed his rightful place on the throne and ruled from Edinburgh Castle. David's successor,

Robert II, granted the townsmen permission to build houses within the castle walls for better protection in times of trouble. And trouble indeed was to come, for the intrigues and power struggles that characterize Scottish political history at this time reached their zenith in Edinburgh – focus of Scottish nationhood and royal court. The infamous Black Dinner of 1440, for example, when the Douglas heir and his brother were dragged away from the table, in front of the young King James II, and beheaded, was one of the more unpleasant incidents (see Threave Castle), and the rivalry between James II and his brother, the Duke of Albany, resulted in them both, successively, finding themselves imprisoned in the castle.

After James II's death the castle was no longer used as a permanent royal residence, although Mary, Queen of Scots gave birth to the future James VI and I here in 1566. After Mary's downfall the castle was held by her supporters, besieged and taken, after which Regent Morton rebuilt its defences and constructed the Half Moon Battery. From this time onwards

Edinburgh became solely a fortress, only occasionally visited by the monarch, but its strategic value was always of paramount importance to both the Scots and the English. In 1650, for instance, the Scots proclaimed Charles II the rightful king in Edinburgh and Cromwell invaded, taking the castle after inflicting extensive damage on it. The final great siege came in the 'Glorious Revolution' which brought William of Orange to the throne; the Duke of Gordon, though instructed by the exiled James VII and II to leave the castle, fought on against English troops until starvation and disease forced his surrender. From then on the castle was used as a fortress (it was one of the four strongholds that were to be fully manned and maintained after the Act of Union in 1707; the others were Stirling, Dumbarton and Blackness), and as a prison (French, Dutch and American prisoners have all languished here).

FEATURES

So varied and violent is Edinburgh's history that little remains of its earlier buildings, with the exception of St Margaret's Chapel. The curtain wall which surrounds the summit dates only from the 17th and 18th centuries, although Morton's Half Moon Battery is older (1574). The 18th century saw the construction of new ranges of defences, including Butt's Battery, the famous six-gun Argyll Battery and the Western Defences. The heart of the castle is higher up the rock and forms a square; the buildings here include the great hall with its astonishing hammer-beam roof, built by James IV for ceremonial occasions and now the repository for the Scottish regalia and home of the United Services Museum. The fourth side of the square is occupied by the Scottish National War Memorial. The wide Esplanade,

scene of the famous annual military tattoo, also recalls two incidents, one brave and one bizarre, that remind us that history is also made up of individual incidents as well as great events. The first is a granite block which commemorates the courage of Ensign Charles Ewart, who seized the French standard at the battle of Waterloo; and the second is a section of ground which is, in legal fiction, Nova Scotian territory, a relic of Charles II's attempts to raise money by granting baronetcies in Nova Scotia; the territory at Edinburgh was used, symbolically, to allow the barons to take formal possession of their property.

⊗ EDZELL CASTLE ⊗

EDZELL, TAYSIDE

The crowning glory of this comparatively unremarkable tower house is its amazing 17th-century garden.

HISTORY

The four-storey, L-plan tower of Edzell was constructed in the early 16th century and later enlarged into a quadrangular court-yard mansion, protected by a curtain wall. The owners and builders at this time were the Lindsays, Earls of Crawford. In 1604 Sir David Lindsay created his particularly ambitious pleas-ance or walled garden, as a result of which he died (in 1610) 'in extraordinary debt'. The Lindsays managed to stay on at Edzell until 1715, when the debts could no longer be forestalled and the estate was sold. The buyer, Lord Panmure, had little time to enjoy his new purchase as he was forced to forfeit the property in punishment for his part in the Stewart Risings. The York Buildings Company then bought the castle and began to dismantle it before themselves becoming bankrupt in 1764. That same year the Earl of Panmure repurchased the estate and it remained in his family's hands until it was taken into state care earlier this century.

FEATURES

The tower of Edzell is the most complete of the buildings although the ruins of the adjacent mansion house suggest that it once would have provided spacious accommodation, with the family rooms on the first floor over domestic offices. It is, how-

ever, the pleasance which makes Edzell special. This beautiful garden (measuring 173 feet by 144 feet) is surrounded by walls 12 feet high which carry a remarkable set of stone panels illustrating the Cardinal Virtues, Liberal Arts and the Celestial Deities. Holes are cut into the walls to hold summer flowers. The neatly trimmed boxwood hedges in the formal garden spell out the Lindsay family motto: Dum spiro spero (While I Breathe I Hope). A bath-house, a rare luxury in the 17th century, stood at one corner and was an elaborate construction with dressing room and sitting room (complete with fireplace). The summerhouse, by contrast, is still in good condition; this too is an elaborate structure, rising two storeys and with its own stair-tower, gunloops and turret.

❀ EILEAN DONAN ❀
CASTLE

DORNIE, HIGHLAND

*M*uch loved by legions of calendar compilers, photogenic Eilean Donan has come to symbolize the very essence of the Highlands of Scotland.

HISTORY

Standing on a remote islet, once accessible only by boat, Eilean Donan overlooks the meeting point of three lochs and is surrounded by tranquil scenery. Perhaps it was a combination of this remoteness and beauty that encouraged the early Celtic saint, Donan, to make his lonely home on the island, later to be named after him. The first major building here was erected in the 13th century by Alexander II to guard against a Viking invasion and this castle later passed to the Mackenzies and then to the MacRaes, who became Constables of the castle in 1506. The two outstanding episodes in Eilean Donan's history both involve sieges. In the first, the MacRaes were defending the castle against the overwhelming forces of Donald Gorm of Sleat in 1539. A fortuitous arrow, his very last, was released by Duncan MacRae, severed an artery in Gorm's foot and thus brought the siege to an end. The outcome of the second siege was, unfortunately, rather more destructive and resulted in the bombardment of the castle by three Royal Navy ships in 1719, in an effort to dislodge a small garrison of Spanish soldiers who had come to Scotland to help James, the Old Pretender, to secure the throne. The medieval castle was no match for the Navy's cannon; after only a few broadsides the Spanish surrendered and Eilean Donan was left, broken and open to the elements, for over two hundred years until it was restored, as accurately as possible, by Lt.Col. John MacRae-Gilstrap. It is now the headquarters of the Clan MacRae.

FEATURES

Eilean Donan's most spectacular feature is, of course, its magnificent natural setting, but the painstaking restoration creates an air of authenticity for all but the most unrelenting purist and there are some fine pieces of furniture, Highland paintings and many clan trophies to see – including, somewhat improbably, cups made from cannonballs!

❈ ELCHO CASTLE ❈

Still owned by the family who built it, this fine fortified mansion on the banks of the Tay has quietly observed 500 years of history pass it by.

HISTORY

The origins of Elcho are somewhat hazy as records have been lost, but it was certainly constructed by the Wemyss family and dates from the 16th century. Although the family was elevated to the peerage in the early 17th century they seem to have played little part in the major political and religious issues of the 17th and 18th centuries and Elcho, as a result, has remained relatively undamaged. The one exception to the Wemyss policy of prudence and caution in state affairs was David, Lord Elcho, and heir to the 5th Earl who, in 1745, joined Bonnie Prince Charlie's forces, fought at Culloden and escaped to France. The title and property then passed to his younger brother who had adopted the surname Charteris. One other important event occurred in 1773 when Elcho, no longer inhabited, was used as a grain store. This was a famine year and starving citizens marched on the castle intending to release the grain. Troops were called out and the citizenry quietly returned to Perth empty-handed.

FEATURES

Although comparatively little known, Elcho is one of Scotland's most interesting castles and is an excellent example of a fortified mansion. Thus, whilst it has several defensive features, its design

shows an equal concern for domestic comfort and convenience. Elcho is, essentially, a central tower house with towers and wings projecting outward. The arrangement of these towers, both square and round and with or without parapet walks, crenellation and turrets, seems rather haphazard and eccentric, but nevertheless is pleasing to the eye and gives Elcho its distinctive character. These defensive features are supported by several strategically placed gunloops, a strong yett (iron gate) at the entrance and iron grilles on all the windows. Domestic and aesthetic concerns are represented by the large kitchen with its huge chimney, the broad stone stairway leading to the main hall which has some remnants of fine plasterwork on the ceiling and three separate stairways to the bedrooms, all of which have a private entrance, fireplace and en suite lavatory with drain!

❊ THE ROYAL PALACE ❊
OF FALKLAND

FALKLAND, FIFE

A royal property since 1402, Falkland will be forever associated with the romantic, yet tragic, Stuart dynasty.

HISTORY

An earlier castle, owned first by the Earls of Fife and ultimately by the ambitious Duke of Albany, was confiscated by King James I. The castle passed to his son, James II, in 1437 and it is his successors, James IV and James V who turned the original tower house into a small palace of some considerable style. James VI used Falkland as a holiday retreat and gifted it to his bride, Anne of Denmark, in 1589. Both Charles I and Charles II stayed at Falkland but, after the end of the Stuart monarchy, and its burning in 1654, Falkland was unused and gradually fell into disrepair. In 1887 the 3rd Marquess of Bute became Custodian and began a programme of restoration which was continued by his successors. In 1952 the National Trust for Scotland was appointed Deputy Keeper.

FEATURES

When work halted on the palace after the death of James V, Falkland was a courtyard structure consisting of three ranges, of which the south range is the best preserved. During James V's reign political links with France became stronger than ever and it is, perhaps, due to this (and the fact that both his wives were French!) that the courtyard side of the south range shows a

strongly Continental influence, including Renaissance columns and windows with medallions. Several of the fittings in the Chapel Royal were installed for Charles II's visit at the time of his 'Scottish' coronation at Scone in 1651; and the colourful ceiling has recently been repainted as accurately as possible. This, and the painstaking and careful restoration of the King's Bedchamber in the Crosshouse, help to bring to life the true spirit of Falkland, in its full flowering as a royal favourite. The real (or royal) tennis courts date from 1539 and are the second oldest in Britain (the oldest are at Hampton), as well as being the only surviving example of their particular form anywhere.

153

⚜ FLOORS CASTLE ⚜

*A*n architectural flight of fancy with its pepper-pot turrets, embattled parapets, corbelling and castellation, rising rather incongruously from the peaceful, sloping hills overlooking the River Tweed and the old market town of Kelso.

HISTORY

Floors is the largest inhabited house in Scotland and the seat of the present 10th Duke of Roxburghe, a member of the long-established and powerful Border family, the Kers. The castle, although it may appear at first sight to be of Tudor origin is not, in fact, old at all. Constructed around an earlier, much more modest 18th-century mansion, the present castle was built by the 6th Duke of Roxburghe, who commissioned the famous 19th-century architect, William Playfair, to transform the mansion into a much grander edifice. Playfair, who is chiefly remembered as the architect whose classical designs, marked by restraint and proportion, helped to transform Edinburgh into the 'Athens of the North', clearly welcomed this opportunity to abandon his customary limitations, and entered into his task with relish. Thus Floors became a 19th-century extravaganza of mock-Tudor decorative features; ostentatious and cluttered it may be, but impossible to ignore!

FEATURES

Externally the castle is much the same as when Playfair completed it, but internally it is much altered. In keeping with a common 19th-century practice amongst the increasingly impoverished members of the British aristocracy, the 8th Duke of Roxburgh married an American heiress, Mary Goelet, in 1892, and the castle subsequently had to be adapted to accommodate the property she brought with her. Ironically, much of the French furniture, European porcelain and splendid tapestries of which 'Duchess May' was so fond, had already crossed the Atlantic once before — having been acquired by the astute Americans during the chaos of the French Revolution. Duchess

May redesigned the ballroom and drawing room in the style of Louis XV to hold her Brussels tapestries and 17th-century French furniture, and one of the tower rooms was transformed into a copy of one at Versailles. There are collections of Chinese and European porcelain and paintings and a Bird Room is devoted to an unusual collection of stuffed birds.

❈ FYVIE CASTLE ❈

FYVIE, GRAMPIAN

The five towers of Fyvie symbolize the five families who have owned it, and encompass over 500 years of Scottish history within their walls.

HISTORY

Fyvie began life as an early 13th-century castle of enclosure, but has been modified so extensively that it is difficult to find any trace of pre-1400 work. Its towers are each named after one of the families who owned the castle, each of whom made their own contribution to its development. Preston Tower dates from the early 15th century and is the oldest surviving part of the castle. The Meldrums then became owners, followed in 1596 by the Setons. Sir Alexander Seton, Lord Fyvie and 1st Earl of Dunfermline, became one of the most influential men in the country and, eventually, Chancellor of Scotland, in 1604. Unfortunately the 4th Earl reversed the family's fortunes by supporting the doomed Jacobite movement and was forced to flee for his life in 1690, leaving Fyvie to revert to the Crown. William Gordon, 2nd Earl of Aberdeen, bought the property some 40 years later and the Gordon family occupied the castle for about a century until financial difficulties compelled them to sell it. Fyvie was then bought by Alexander Leith, later Lord Leith, a local man who had made a fortune in American steel. Fyvie was acquired by the National Trust for Scotland in 1984.

FEATURES

Externally, Fyvie is a superb example of Scots baronial architecture at its most powerful and confidant; the immense central gatehouse tower in the south front, for example, complemented by the two square, cone-capped towers at each end. Inside, the accumulated treasures of five centuries include fine furniture, tapestries, paintings, arms and armour. Perhaps the most striking feature here is the magnificent sweeping wheel-stair, the finest in Scotland, installed by the 1st Earl of Dunfermline. These graceful, 10-foot-wide steps were, however, treated with scant respect by later owners, the Gordons, who are reputed to have ridden their horses up the staircase for a wager! The morning room has a superb 17th-century plaster ceiling and panelling and the 20th century is well represented by Lord Leith's opulent Edwardian interiors.

✶ GIRNIGOE CASTLE ✶

WICK, HIGHLAND

*I*ts name once synonymous with terror, the desolate ruins of Girnigoe still rise spectacularly from the very edge of a rocky promontory,

HISTORY

The castle was built in the late 15th century as the stronghold of the Sinclairs, Earls of Caithness, who sallied forth regularly to harry the inhabitants of the North with their lawlessness and brutality. Indeed, their cruelty extended to members of their own family and George, the 4th Earl, even went so far as to imprison his son and heir, John, in Girnigoe for seven years on suspicion of 'treachery'. Finally, so it is said, the earl gave John salt beef to eat (but nothing to drink). Inevitably his son died a terrible death, having first lost his mind. Incredibly, this same earl was Justiciar of Caithness and the story illustrates just how much power such individuals could exercise far from the centre of law and government. The unfortunate John's son, George, who succeeded to the title, proved to be a wild and quarrelsome man himself and spent most of his life hatching plots and fighting his neighbours, until he died, bankrupt, in 1643. The castle was later claimed by Sir John Campbell of Glenorchy in lieu of debts, but this was disputed by the Sinclair heir. Sinclair of Keiss, using the disputed title as an excuse, besieged Girnigoe and defeated the resident branch of the Sinclairs in 1679. The castle was ruined by 1700.

FEATURES

The castle, with its towering seaward walls rising vertically from the brink of the cliff, is essentially a late 15th-century tower house and two wings, designed on an E-shaped plan with a double courtyard. A further development, situated across a gap in the cliff, was constructed around 1606 and is sometimes described as a separate castle, Castle Sinclair. Girnigoe is protected on the landward side by a ditch some 15 feet deep and 15 feet wide. Although little of the interior remains to be seen, the tall, gaunt walls are impressive, swept always by the cold sea winds which, even on a sunny day, chill the air and, perhaps, remind us of more savage times.

❧ GLAMIS CASTLE ❧

GLAMIS, TAYSIDE

Famous as the fictional home of Shakespeare's Macbeth and as the real childhood home of the Queen Mother, Glamis has been likened to both a French chateau and a Walt Disney cartoon!

HISTORY

Glamis is the family home of the Earls of Strathmore and Kinghorne and has been in the Lyon family since King Robert II gave the lands to his Keeper of the Privy Seal, Sir John Lyon, in 1372 on Sir John's marriage to Robert's daughter. The Lyon connection with royalty did not always bring good fortune however. The wife of the 6th Lord Glamis was burned at the stake with the full knowledge and encouragement of James V, who suspected her of treachery. Her son, the heir and 7th Lord, was also condemned to death but, being too young, was kept prisoner until he was of an age to be executed! The Lyon estates meanwhile were forfeited. Some time later the accuser confessed that the charges against Lady Glamis and her son were false, but the young lord was not released and his property restored until after the death of James V. On a lighter note, the 3rd Earl of Strathmore and Kinghorne was reputedly the last man in the country to employ a jester – although legend has it that the man was dismissed after becoming too attached to the earl's daughter!

FEATURES

The 14th-century Sir John Lyon constructed a strong tower house, rising to four storeys and ending with battlements. This

now forms the core of the present castle and probably incorporates fragments of an even older building. In the 17th century major remodelling work was undertaken, during which the tower was heightened and roofed, a new entrance was made and two new wings were added. As the importance of defensive considerations declined, owners and builders could indulge their more creative fantasies and Glamis, with its proliferation of bartizans, cone-capped turrets and crenellations, is an excellent example of this trend. In 1767 the 9th Earl married an English heiress, Mary Eleanor Bowes, and changed the family name to Bowes-Lyon. The castle has remained in the family by direct descent since the 14th century. It is packed with treasures, including royal and family portraits, fine furnishings, porcelain, armour and tapestries, all displayed in sumptuous settings.

❈ GLENBUCHAT CASTLE ❈

GLENBUCHAT, GRAMPIAN

A fine example of a late 16th-century military stronghold, forever associated with the vivid life of the last Gordon laird.

HISTORY

Glenbuchat was built by John Gordon the Younger of Cairnbarrow and his second wife, Helen Carnegie, in 1590. Their names, now almost illegible, were carved above the entrance door, together with the stern admonition that 'No thing on Arth remanis bot faime'. And 'fame' certainly came to the Gordons through one of their successors, another John Gordon – 'Old Glenbuchat' as he came to be known. The Gordons were always strong supporters of the Stuart line and the Gordon laird was 'out' for the Pretenders in both the 1715 and 1745 Jacobite Risings. After 1715 Old Glenbuchat spent some time in an Edinburgh prison but he remained loyal to the Stuarts on his release, eventually becoming one of Prince Charles's principal advisers. At the battle of Culloden (1746), Old Glenbuchat (at the age of 68) was in the forefront of the fighting and commanded the Farquharsons and the Gordons. After the prince's defeat all the Gordon lands were forfeited and Old Glenbuchat became a fugitive, sleeping in the hills and 'living rough' through the long Highland winters. Despite the astronomical ransom of £1000 which was offered for his capture, he was never betrayed and finally, at the age of 70, he made his way to the coast and escaped to Norway, then to

Sweden. He died, penniless, in Boulogne in 1750. Glenbuchat was eventually bought by the Earl of Fife.

FEATURES

Glenbuchat, though ruined, is nevertheless still an excellent model of the classic late 16th-century Z-plan military stronghold, with two diagonally opposite towers (complete with turrets), guardroom and a plentiful supply of gunloops. One of the most unusual features of the castle is that the stairs, in the large angle stair turrets which rise from the first floor level, are supported by arches rather than the more usual corbels, a feature more usually found in French buildings of this period. It is known that Helen Carnegie's father travelled in France and it is possible that this French influence is derived from him.

❈ HAILES CASTLE ❈

EAST LINTON, LOTHIAN

A romantic ruin overlooking the Scottish River Tyne and for-ever associated with the vigorous and brave, if foolhardy and headstrong, Hepburn family.

HISTORY

The oldest parts of the castle date back to the 13th century when the Earl of Dunbar erected a small courtyard castle, almost a fortified manor, on the site. By the end of the 14th century the castle was enlarged by the Hepburns who also added a great square tower and a massive curtain wall, almost nine feet thick and strengthened with towers. In 1388 the then laird and his son, Patrick, valiantly prevented the banner of Douglas from falling into English hands at the battle of Otterburn. In another feat of derring-do a later Hepburn, the 4th Earl of Bothwell, 'abducted' Mary, Queen of Scots in April 1567 and brought her here to Hailes on their way to Dunbar Castle; he soon became Mary's third husband. But the Hepburns were by no means only 'men of action'; some scions of the family were men of consider-able intellect and achieved high office such as Bishop of Brechin and Prior of St Andrews. Hailes was partly destroyed by Cromwell in 1650 and the remains were sold to David Dalrymple, Lord Hailes, in the 18th century.

FEATURES

The most remarkable aspect of Hailes, apart from its beautiful setting, is the substantial quantity of 13th-century masonry still

in place; this is found mainly in the lower sections of the walls, particularly those on the eastern side; 14th- and 15th-century additions are on the western side. The northern range, along the riverside, dates mainly from the 14th century and includes a postern stair, ribbed and vaulted, leading to the river. About halfway down there is a landing, once protected by a drawbridge and a deep pit. The lower part of the stair was probably wooden and movable. There are two particularly gruesome pit prisons at Hailes – one in each of the remaining towers – with narrow air shafts and drains angled through the massive walls.

✹ HERMITAGE CASTLE ✹

A grim and forbidding edifice, its massive walls rising abruptly from the bleak, marshy ground at the head of Liddesdale valley and overlooking Hermitage Water. As a key stronghold in the much fought-over Borders region, Hermitage, the 'strength of Liddesdale', has a gruesome and cruel history.

HISTORY

The grisly history of Hermitage begins with the building of an earlier, possibly 13th-century castle, whose owner, Lord de Soulis, was captured by the local inhabitants and reputedly boiled alive in a cauldron for his misdeeds. Later becoming the property of the Douglas family, the castle was the scene of the miserable death of Sir Alexander Ramsay, systematically starved by his opponent, Sir William Douglas. (You can still see the five-foot by six-foot pit prison where Ramsay ended his days, having survived for over two weeks on grain slipping through cracks in the ceiling from the granary overhead.) The Douglases lost possession of Hermitage, briefly, to the English, who built a fortified manor house on the castle site, converted by the Douglases into a tower house in 1371. James IV, uneasy that the unruly and rebellious Douglas family held a stronghold of such strategic importance, forced an exchange of castles between the Douglas and Bothwell families. It was to Hermitage, to visit her lover, the Earl of Bothwell, injured in a Borders brawl, that Mary, Queen of Scots rode from Jedburgh in October 1566. The 40-mile round trip made her so ill that it almost cost her

her life; much later, when tragedy overtook her, she would say, sadly, 'Would that I had died at Jedburgh'. In 1587 Hermitage was granted by James VI to Bothwell's nephew, Francis Stewart, through whom it passed to the Buccleuch family.

FEATURES

Today, extensively restored externally, Hermitage is an outstanding example of a medieval Border castle with its keep, four corner towers connected by flying arches, and corbelled parapet. It was intended strictly as a fortress, with its defence depending not on position but on the difficulty of dragging cumbersome siege machinery up the dale, the permanently marshy ground and the sheer impregnability of its massive walls.

✸ HUNTINGTOWER ✸
CASTLE
PERTH, TAYSIDE

A well-restored fortified house, seat of the powerful and ambitious Ruthven family, Earls of Gowrie, whose political intrigues finally led to their downfall.

HISTORY

Huntingtower was originally known as Ruthven Castle and consisted, surprisingly, of two 15th-century tower houses standing just over nine feet apart, connected only by a movable wooden bridge at parapet level. The reason for this is not certain, but may be have been for defensive purposes – the second tower being a safe refuge in the event of the first one being breached, for instance. In the late 16th century the two towers were united by a lower, three-storey block. The Ruthvens were extremely active in Scottish politics throughout the 16th century and, in 1581, Lord Ruthven was made the 1st Earl of Gowrie. In 1582 the insecure and adolescent James VI accepted a pressing 'invitation' to stay at Ruthven Castle – later known as the Ruthven Raid – and was kept prisoner there for 10 months until he escaped from his guards while out hunting. In retaliation the Earl of Gowrie was captured and beheaded in 1585. James, however, had an extremely long memory and in 1600 the 3rd and last Earl of Gowrie, with his brother, Alexander, were murdered in Perth under the pretence that they were plotting against the king (the so-called Gowrie Conspiracy). The Gowrie lands were forfeited and their name abolished. The castle was renamed

Huntingtower and remained royal property until 1643 when Charles I gave it to William Murray, Earl Dysart and Lord Huntingtower. It is now in the care of the state.

FEATURES

The original tower is at the eastern end of the building and was erected in the early 15th century. The hall on the first floor has some fine black and white painted wooden ceilings, dating from the mid-16th century. The second tower was probably built in the later years of that century. The gap between the towers is known as the Maiden's Leap – the tradition being that the 1st Earl's daughter, about to be caught with her (unsuitable) lover in one tower, leapt across the gap and back to her own room before being trapped. Presumably the maiden decided that one leap was enough, because the next night she eloped with, and married, her beloved!

✠ HUNTLY CASTLE ✠

Huntly, Grampian

*H*untly is a history lesson in stone – the centuries of destruction, rebuilding and alteration paralleling the varying fortunes of its powerful and ambitious Gordon owners.

HISTORY

There has been a castle at Huntly (originally called Strathbogie) since the 12th century, and a simple Norman motte-and-bailey structure stood on the site when Robert the Bruce gave the lands at Strathbogie to Sir Adam Gordon of Huntly in the 14th century. The family continued to prosper and in the 1436 the Gordons became Earls of Huntly. It is probably around this time that they decided to build a grander residence for themselves to conform with their rising social status. The 1st Earl of Huntly died in 1470 and the building was completed by his son. By this time the Gordons had become very influential and their new castle was often visited by men and women of status and distinction. In 1506 the castle was renamed Huntly and later that century the 4th Earl (the proud 'Cock o' the North') began an extensive building programme. Both the 4th and 5th Earls took up arms against their monarchs (Mary, Queen of Scots and James VI) and both were defeated, thus closing the era of Gordon power and leading to the castle's destruction in 1594. In 1597, however, the 5th Earl made peace with the king, became 1st Marquess and began another rebuilding programme. The 2nd Marquess remained loyal to King Charles I for which he was executed, and Huntly was again destroyed. After the Civil War the castle was abandoned by the Gordons.

FEATURES

The remains of Huntly today are mainly remnants of the rebuilding programmes of the 4th and 5th Earls in the 16th and 17th centuries. The massive round tower symbolizes Gordon strength and the elegant row of oriel windows expresses the artistic and aesthetic concerns of a noble family. Beneath the castle is a 15th-century dungeon, approached by a narrow passage, its walls covered with 16th-century graffiti. The splendid carved heraldic doorway is one of the finest in the country.

❈ INVERARAY CASTLE ❈

*A*n eccentric 18th-century fantasy, the Highland retreat of the rich and powerful Campbells, Dukes of Argyll.

HISTORY

When Archibald, the 3rd Duke, conceived the idea of constructing a brand-new castle for himself, he also decided to rebuild the entire village of Inveraray at the same time. Unlike the castle, however, the village was reconstructed along classical lines, giving it an air of proportion and restraint, qualities which are, perhaps, in shorter supply at the castle itself. Inveraray was finally completed by the 5th Duke in 1770 and both village and castle soon became an essential stopover on the newly emergent Highland tourist trail. (Dr Johnson, Robert Burns and John Keats all stayed at the Great Inn in the village.) The castle is still the seat of the Clan Chief, the Duke of Argyll, and is also the worldwide clan centre.

FEATURES

The castle, constructed from blue-grey stone, is, externally, a rather unsatisfactory mixture of neo-Gothic and neo-Scots baronial features: the square shape of the castle, for example, its corner towers and battlements indicate Scots baronial influence, whilst the pointed and mullioned windows are neo-Gothic. In addition, a major reconstruction of the castle was carried out after a serious fire in 1877 and this led to further alterations and additions by Anthony Salin. The rather incongruous central

tower, which is constructed of a different material and appears to be slowly sinking behind the front facade, is one such addition. Internally, however, the castle is gracious and well proportioned, the work of Robert Mylne, commissioned by the 5th Duke in 1772, and is characterized by fine ceiling plasterwork, painted wall panels and superb wood carving. Of particular note are the family portraits, collections of porcelain and furniture, including 18th-century Beauvais tapestries, and 10 sets of gilded chairs, several of these also covered by Beauvais tapestries.

INVERGARRY CASTLE

INVERGARRY, HIGHLAND

A remote, haunting ruin, this erstwhile chieftain's stronghold stands on the steep banks of Loch Oich, surrounded by some of the most truly spectacular scenery in Scotland.

HISTORY

Invergarry Castle was, for centuries, the Highland seat and fortress of the MacDonnells of Glengarry, and at least two castles were built and destroyed before the present building. The first was dismantled by the Parliamentary forces of General Monck in 1654 and the second was burned down in 1689. Prince Charles Edward Stuart visited the present castle twice, for which it was burned and destroyed in revenge by the Duke of Cumberland ('Butcher Cumberland') in 1746. A curious story is associated with Invergarry and tells of an episode that took place in the 17th century and is commemorated by a monument a short distance from the castle. The story involves Keppoch, the chief of a branch of the MacDonnells, who sent his two sons to France to be educated. When Keppoch died he left his affairs in the hands of his seven brothers, who, on the young heirs' return from France, promptly murdered them and claimed their inheritance. The family bard (or poet) then took his revenge by murdering the brothers themselves, removing their heads and, having first washed them in a well, The Well of the Heads, took them to the clan chief at Invergarry. An inscription on the well, in Gaelic, French and English, commends his 'ample and summary vengeance'!

FEATURES

Although ruinous, enough can be seen of this once-great strong-hold, still towering over the tranquil waters of the loch to indicate a castle of considerable size and strength. Built on an L-shaped plan, and designed for safety rather than comfort, the 17th-century remains indicate that the principal building was five storeys high. The spacious hall on the first floor (45 feet by 22 feet) and the generous proportions of the other buildings suggest that Invergarry was once a worthy residence for the Clan Chief. The castle now stands in the grounds of a hotel.

❈ KELBURN CASTLE ❈

FAIRLIE, STRATHCLYDE

The ancestral seat of the Earls of Glasgow, Kelburn commands breathtaking views across the Firth of Clyde and across to the Cumbrae Islands, Arran and Bute.

HISTORY

When William the Conqueror came to England in 1066 he brought with him many noble and ambitious Norman French families, one of which was the de Boyvilles, later Boyle. In time, Norman power and influence spread northwards into Scotland, where the Scottish kings welcomed the newcomers, seeing an opportunity to create a strong and loyal power base. To this end, large areas of land were gifted by the kings to the newly-arrived Normans to encourage their fidelity, and this is how the lands at Kelburn came into the hands of the de Boyvilles in the late 12th century. The Boyles quickly became part of the established order and continued to prosper; in 1699 David Boyle was created Lord Boyle of Kelburn and, in 1703, he became the Earl of Glasgow. The Earl was a man of considerable wealth and influence (he was actively involved in the promotion of the Act of Union which united the governments of England and Scotland in 1707) and, evidently feeling that the old castle at Kelburn no longer befitted his rising social status, erected a fine new mansion house next to the older building. An additional wing was constructed in 1870 and the castle is still owned and occupied by the present Earl and Countess of Glasgow.

Features

The oldest part of the castle is the stone tower house which dates back to the 13th century, but the building which we see today consists mainly of 16th-century additions to the tower (which almost doubled the size of the castle), plus a large 17th-century mansion. No attempt was made to incorporate the mansion into the existing building (see Brodick Castle, for example), and the building lies at an angle to the older structure. However the 'new' building has an attractive symmetry and is a fine example of an early 18th-century country mansion. The gardens contain several unusual species such as as the weeping larch, and the yews are thought to be 1000 years old.

❊ KELLIE CASTLE ❊

PITTENWEEM, FIFE

A fine Scots baronial mansion house, its stern simplicity mellowed by beautiful surroundings and an enchanting garden.

HISTORY

Kellie was built by the Oliphant family in about 1360 and sold in 1613 to Thomas Erskine, later the 1st Earl of Kellie. Alterations and extensions over the years transformed Kellie into a fine Scots baronial mansion, but this did not prevent it from being abandoned in 1830 and left open to the depradations of wind and weather. That the castle survived at all is due to the love and care bestowed upon it by Professor James Lorimer (father of the famous architect, Sir Robert Lorimer) who, from 1878, undertook to repair and restore Kellie as an 'improving tenant'. Lorimer's Latin inscription on the wall testifies to the hard work and devotion he committed to the restoration of Kellie: 'This mansion, snatched from rooks and owls, is dedicated to honest ease amidst labours'. In 1937, however, there was a 'muckle roup' or sale of the contents, after which the castle was again abandoned. Once more, however, the Lorimer family came to the rescue: Hew Lorimer, a grandson of the professor, and his wife, rented and then bought the property. Their devotion to Kellie's improvement and preservation equalled that of the professor and the castle became alive once again. In 1970 Kellie was bought for the nation, together with most of its contents, and is now owned and cared for by the National Trust for Scotland, who have also restored the very pretty formal garden.

FEATURES

The present structure is a fine illustration of 16th- and 17th-century domestic architecture and consists of two 16th-century towers joined by a 17th-century range. The typical Scots baronial features of crow-stepped gables, dormer windows, moulded chimney copes and corbelling are all present. Inside, the painted panelling in the diningroom is of interest: there are 64 panels, each showing an improbably romantic scene – crashing waves, rocky promontories, fortresses, mighty waterfalls and so on. The ceiling of the Vine Room, a richly-worked representation of vine leaves and fruit, is particularly well executed.

❈ KILDRUMMY CASTLE ❈

One of the most powerful medieval castles in northern Scotland and a much fought-over prize.

HISTORY

Built on behalf of Alexander II in the early 13th century to control Mar and Moray and the route between them, Kildrummy's strategic position inevitably made it a coveted trophy in the constant power struggles that, for centuries, dominated the area's history. In the early 14th century, for example, Kildrummy was under the control of Edward I of England, who ordered alterations to strengthen its fortifications – a step he must have regretted taking some three years later, in 1306, when, the castle having fallen into the hands of Robert the Bruce's supporters, proved to be impregnable to his own troops! Treachery, however, won the day for the king, and the blacksmith, Osbourne, who had deliberately set fire to the castle in return for all the English gold he could carry, had it poured down his throat in a molten stream instead of given to him in bags as he had anticipated. Kildrummy was besieged once again in 1335, but the following century Sir Alexander Stewart devised a less time-consuming method of gaining ownership by seizing its unfortunate owner, the Countess of Mar, and forcing her to marry him. Once again, in 1654, Kildrummy was besieged, but this time its 300-year-old walls were no match for Cromwell's cannon and it quickly fell. The castle was deliberately damaged by the Jacobites in 1670 to prevent it from being used by the government and, after the 1715 Rising, dismantled and used as a quarry.

FEATURES

Kildrummy was planned as a mighty, defensive stronghold, protected by a steep ravine on one side, an extensive semi-circular curtain wall and a wide, deep ditch on the others. The wall was defended by five projecting round towers, one of which served as a keep – the final refuge for defenders. Edward I added a massive gatehouse, with two round (drum) towers. Although much ruined, the sheer size and strength of Kildrummy, the 'noblest of northern castles' is, nevertheless, still intimidating.

❊ KISIMUL CASTLE ❊

CASTLEBAY, ISLE OF BARRA, WESTERN ISLES

The story of Kisimul is as romantic as any Highland myth and embraces almost a thousand years of history and the fulfilment of a 20th-century American dream.

HISTORY

The earliest castle here was constructed by the MacNeils of Barra as their stronghold and clan seat, in about 1030. The MacNeils were a proud and fearless family, claiming descent from the Irish King Niall of the Nine Hostages. Such noble ancestry did not, however, preclude the MacNeils from becoming notorious pirates, harrying shipping mercilessly in the western seas. (You can still see where they berthed their great ship, a possession which, so the tale goes, prompted a clan member to say, in response to Noah's invitation to the Clan Chief to take up a place on his ark, 'The MacNeil has a boat of his own!') By the late 18th and early 19th centuries, however, the MacNeil fortunes had declined so much that they abandoned Barra and went to America. In 1938 the then Clan Chief, Robert Lister MacNeil, an American architect, began at last to realize his dream of restoring Kisimul and the work was completed in the early 1960s.

FEATURES

The walls of Kisimul were shaped to fit the contours of the islet on which it stands in Castlebay, thus making it extremely difficult to attack, particularly as the islet is almost submerged at

high tide, and water laps the castle walls. Early buildings within
the curtain wall would be simple thatched constructions, including a watchtower, great hall and accommodation for the galley's
crew, as well as a chapel. The dominant feature is the 14th-cen-
tury Great Tower, five storeys high, which contained a room for
the garrison and the Chief's lodging, with access via a movable
wooden platform and an outside stair.

BARNTON, EDINBURGH, LOTHIAN

$\mathcal{A}$ gracious and elegant residence, now a fascinating museum dedicated to late Victorian and Edwardian taste.

HISTORY

Lauriston is based on a 16th-century tower house, built by Sir Archibald Napier (whose son, John, invented logarithms), and was sold, in 1656, to Charles II's solicitor, Robert Dalgleish. In 1683 the castle was again sold, this time to an Edinburgh gold-smith, William Law, and subsequently became the home of John Law, the colourful banker who, astonishingly, became Comptroller General of the finances of France. Unfortunately, whatever financial acumen John Law possessed did not extend to the management of his personal resources and he achieved a breathtaking bankruptcy, dying in poverty in Venice in 1729. From 1827 onwards the castle underwent several changes of ownership and acquired substantial additions designed by such distinguished architects as William Burn and W H Playfair. The last private owners, Mr and Mrs Reid, bequeathed the house and its contents to the people of the city of Edinburgh in 1919, on condition that it should be left as it was.

FEATURES

The original rectangular tower had three storeys and an attic, topped by two large turrets, and remained substantially unaltered from the 16th century until the 19th century neo-Jacobean additions. The south front bears the initials of the builder, Sir Alexander Napier, and his second wife, Dame Elizabeth Moubray, in addition to the names of Robert Dalgleish and his wife, Jean Douglas. The principal room in the old house is the Oak Room, complete with secret staircase and hidden chamber, supplied with convenient listening hole and spyhole for effective 16th-century 'bugging'! The last owners were avid collectors and their home is filled with furniture and objets-d'art, including a fine collection of

Derbyshire Blue John ornaments. Above all, however, Lauriston is a time-capsule of late Victorian and Edwardian life, of the gracious elegance of the life once lived there and that would be swept away forever by World War I.

❈ LOCH DOON CASTLE ❈

DALMELLINGTON, STRATHCLYDE

*R*emote and mysterious, this 14th-century ruin stands in wild
and mountainous country beside the cold waters of Loch Doon.

HISTORY

Loch Doon Castle was originally constructed on a rocky islet in
the loch itself – giving it excellent protection from attack. (It
was rebuilt on its present site after the water level of the loch
was raised by about 20 feet in the 1930s as part of a hydro-elec-
tric scheme.) The castle's history is not well documented but it
is thought to have been built by the Earls of Carrick in the early
14th century. It was to this castle, hoping for refuge, that Sir
Christopher Seton fled, hotly pursued by the English, after the
defeat of his lord, Robert the Bruce, at Methven in 1306. Sir
Gilbert de Carrick, the governor of the castle, taking the part of
expediency over courage, surrendered both castle and Sir
Christopher to his enemies; Sir Christopher was hanged as a
traitor at Dumfries but Sir Gilbert managed somehow to restore
himself to royal favour and received a letter of remission from
Robert the Bruce, now King Robert I. Some time later, when
Edward Balliol, usurper of the Scottish throne and puppet of
Edward I, invaded Scotland and took large stretches of land,
Loch Doon was one of the few castles to remain loyal to the
rightful king, David II, son of King Robert I, and was held for
the king by John Thomson, a soldier of fortune, in 1333. Little
more is known of the castle's subsequent history, except that it is

supposed to have been deliberately destroyed by fire, as were several other strongholds in the area, on the orders of James V who hoped, by this rather drastic move, to reduce the powers of the feudal barons, thereby augmenting his own.

FEATURES

Perhaps the castle's best feature is its picturesque lochside situation, encircled by the lonely, windswept hills of Ayrshire. Of particular interest, however, is Loch Doon's very fine pointed arch gateway, 9 feet wide, which was once defended by a strong portcullis, now, reputedly, at the bottom of the loch; an attempt many years ago to raise it when the loch froze over failed when the ice broke under its weight and it sank again. The remains of a tall tower house can still be seen at low water. The curtain wall (which originally followed the contours of the islet, still visible when the water level is low), rose to 26 feet and was up to 9 feet thick in places. Only the curtain wall was rebuilt in the 1930s on the new site.

⚜ LOCH LEVEN CASTLE ⚜

A strong, compact tower standing on an island in the loch, and much used as a grim state prison.

HISTORY

The present building (a replacement for a 13th-century original), erected by the Douglas family of Loch Leven, dates from the 15th century and would, originally, have encompassed the whole island, making attack extremely difficult (although on one occasion English attackers attempted to damn the River Leven and raise the water level sufficiently to drown the inhabitants). The loch was lowered in the 19th century, increasing the surface of the island as we see it today. The strong defensive position and isolation of the castle made it ideal for use as a prison and its Douglas owners, always deeply enmeshed in the intrigues and power struggles of Scottish politics, raised no objections. The most famous prisoner at Loch Leven was, of course, Mary, Queen of Scots, who was brought here on the orders of the Protestant Lords of the Congregation, after her defeat at the battle of Carberry Hill in June 1567. Under the unsympathetic supervision of the castle's owner, Sir William Douglas, Mary's health declined and she became very ill even, so it is said, miscarrying the twins she was expecting. In spite of her condition, however, the noble lords continued to threaten and intimidate her (she was still only 25) and, just over a month later, in July 1567, Mary became so unnerved by the behaviour of Lord Lindsay ('the rudest, most bigoted and fiercest' of them all [Scott]), that she signed a Deed of Abdication in favour of her infant son, making her half-brother, the Earl of Moray, Regent. Over the next few months many attempts were made to rescue Mary and she did, finally, escape in May 1568 with the aid of a 16-year-old Douglas kinsman, William, who had, like many others, become greatly attached to the beautiful and charming ex-queen.

FEATURES

Although much of the castle has been lost, the strong five-storey 15th-century tower, with its five-foot-thick walls and bartizans, has been well preserved, albeit roofless, together with a curtain wall and a smaller, round tower, probably from the 16th century. Originally access to the main tower would have been via a movable wooden staircase and into the second floor above the basement floor (several feet above ground level), which is most unusual. The only access to the first floor was by an internal stair from the second floor; a hatch gave access from the basement to the first floor.

⚜ LOCHMABEN CASTLE ⚜

$\mathcal{T}$he hereditary castle of the Bruces, ruined Lochmaben was once the most powerful fortress in the Borders.

HISTORY

The Lordship of Annandale was given to the Anglo-Norman de Brus (Bruce) family by King David I in the early 12th century, although their earlier stronghold was not built here but at Castlehill nearby. The present castle dates from the 1330s. Because of its proximity to England and the fact that it guarded the routes into south-west Scotland, Lochmaben was much coveted by the English and particularly by Edward I, who took the castle in 1298 and strengthened its defences. Between then and the late 14th century ownership of the castle alternated between England and Scotland. By the middle of the 15th century it was, once and for all, in Scottish hands and, in fact, was a royal castle, much favoured by James IV. Mary, Queen of Scots also stayed here in 1565 with her second husband, Lord Darnley. Lochmaben is known to have survived intact into the 17th century when it was allowed to fall into ruin, the stone quarried for use in local buildings.

FEATURES

It takes some effort of the imagination for the visitor to accept that the ivy-clad fragments of lochside Lochmaben, surrounded by the remains of earthworks, was once an immensely powerful castle, covering almost 16 acres and protected by four concentric

moats! However the ruins are still haunted by traces of their
former glory and are worth visiting for their association with the
great Robert the Bruce, who is reputed to have been born here,
although this is disputed by some authorities. There is a statue
of the Scottish patriot and king in nearby Lochmaben itself, a
quiet little Border town, and the church still has the original
14th-century bell, known as Bruce's bell.

❋ LOCHNAW CASTLE ❋

LESWALT, DUMFRIES & GALLOWAY

*A*n attractive castle set in pretty gardens which run down to the edge of the loch.

HISTORY

Lochnaw was, for 300 years, the home of the Agnew family, hereditary Sheriffs of Galloway, although the present castle dates back only to the 16th century. The Agnews' earlier residence, situated on an islet in the loch itself (fragments remain), was captured and destroyed in 1390 by Archibald Douglas or 'Archibald the Grim' (see Threave Castle). The small tower house was the first section to be built and additions were made in the 17th century, converting the castle first into an L-shape, then U-shape. Later 18th- and 19th-century additions were demolished earlier this century bringing the castle more in line with its 17th-century appearance.

FEATURES

Lochnaw is a most appealing castle, its four-storey small, square tower topped by a picturesque caphouse and watchroom with crow-stepped gables. Just beside the caphouse the parapet is broken by a bottomless projection or machicolation, which was used to drop missiles or boiling liquids on unwelcome visitors. On the east parapet a second projection has been corbelled out to take the passage round the chimney, thus allowing the lookout to gain access right round the castle. Inside, the tower house followed the usual plan of having one room on each floor

and the original moulded fireplaces and aumbries (recesses) have been well preserved. The 17th-century additions form a comfortable three-storey mansion house and were erected by Sir Andrew Agnew and his wife, Anna, daughter of the Earl of Galloway. The dormer windows carry their initials, the Stewart arms and the date, 1663. A further inscription, Dom Andreas Agnew 1426 Nomen Fortissima Turris, is known to be false, although the date is significant in that it is the year that the Douglases (who had destroyed the Agnews' original castle) resigned the Bailiery of Leswalt back to the Agnews.

❈ LOCHRANZA CASTLE ❈

Isle of Arran, Strathclyde

$\mathcal{A}$ picturesque ruin watching over a quiet bay at the northern end of the lovely Isle of Arran.

History

The ruins that we see today date from the 16th century, although there was certainly an earlier structure on the site; Robert the Bruce is reputed to have stayed at Lochranza in 1306 en route from Ireland to the Scottish mainland for the start of his campaign for Scottish independence, and the chronicler, Fordun, writing in the late 14th or early 15th century notes that there are two royal castles on Arran, 'Brethwyk (see Brodick Castle) and Lochransie'. Later the castle became a popular hunting lodge for the Stuart kings. In the 17th century the castle was garrisoned by Cromwell's forces during the Civil Wars, though, unusually, not destroyed by the departing soldiers. Lochranza was bought by the Duchess of Hamilton in 1705 but by the end of that century it was deserted and already falling into decay.

Features

Lochranza is an L-plan castle with a three-storey main block and a square tower rising two storeys higher; this would have been topped by a crenellated parapet and watchtower. The basement of the tower was probably the dungeon, about 7 feet square and 10 feet high. The main block contained the vaulted kitchen and great hall, with raised dais for the laird, on the same level and divided by a partition, broken by a connecting serving hatch. The west tower has a corbelled and machicolated device over the door, used for dropping missiles or boiling liquids on the heads of unwelcome visitors.

❈ MACLELLAN'S CASTLE ❈

KIRKCUDBRIGHT, DUMFRIES & GALLOWAY

*L*ooming over the pleasant streets of this ancient royal burgh are the lofty ruins of Sir Thomas MacLellan's imposing mansion.

HISTORY

Having acquired the lands and property that once belonged to the Franciscan Greyfriars Monastery in 1569, Sir Thomas MacLellan of Bombie, Provost of Kirkcudbright, began to construct his elaborate mansion. Clearly a man of substance and ambition, Sir Thomas married Dame Grizel Maxwell, daughter of Lord Herries, and their son, Sir Robert, became a Gentleman of the Bedchamber to both James VI and Charles I, who knighted him in 1633. The family loyalty to the Crown was, however, eventually to cost the MacLellans their home and fortunes. The 3rd Lord Kirkcudbright was a great soldier and committed both his life and fortune to the Royalist cause, losing what remained in the family coffers after the Restoration by fighting against the Covenanters (those who opposed the king's religious policies). The castle was abandoned by the MacLellans who could no longer afford to live there (one 18th century Lord Kirkcudbright met by Robert Burns ran a glove shop in Edinburgh!). The castle is now in the care of the state.

FEATURES

Although roofless and much ruined inside, MacLellan's Castle still retains its lordly air. In shape it is a very large, traditional, L-shaped fortified house, bearing many of the usual defensive features such as angle turrets and gunloops. However there are

several other details which indicate that MacLellan's was built in a transitional period, a time when Scottish architecture was moving away from predominantly defensive considerations and towards more emphasis on domestic comfort and aesthetic appeal. Here, for instance, there is still the single small entrance door, but it is embellished by three large heraldic panels, two of which bear the arms of MacLellan and Maxwell, the initials GM and the date, 1582. Inside, the castle is spacious and well designed with domestic comfort and convenience given a high priority. The kitchen, for example, is equipped with a stone sink and drain, a door into the courtyard and a vast fireplace; the well-lit great hall is over 42 feet long and, again, has a huge fire-place (the lintel is as much as 11 feet long and carved out of a single stone). A spyhole behind the fireplace leads into a tiny chamber for the spy – who must frequently have become totally immobilised by the smoke!

✺ MEGGINCH CASTLE ✺

ERROL, TAYSIDE

Occupied by the same family since the 17th century, Megginch is a much loved and cared-for family home with beautiful gardens.

HISTORY

Megginch (a corruption of the Gaelic Maol-ginch, 'bare island'), though enfolded now by rich farmland and woodland was actually built on an island in the midst of marsh and bog, thus giving it excellent protection from attack. Its builders, the Hays, were a rich and powerful family and their castle, a pleasing example of Scots baronial style, well supplied with turrets, crenellation and towers, was begun in the late 16th century, as the Latin inscription over one of the windows testifies. In the 1640s, however, the Hays were forced to sell Megginch and it was bought by the colourful and enterprising Drummonds, who still live there. The 3rd Drummond of Megginch was the first local Member of Parliament in the new (and unpopular) United Kingdom Parliament of 1707. The Drummonds were great travellers, often voyaging to such far-flung places as India and China in the days when this was no easy matter. Always, however, they have come home to Megginch and its gardens, loved and cherished by the family through the centuries.

FEATURES

The castle today incorporates an earlier 16th-century tower, strongly fortified and with the usual gunloops and arrow slits in

the turrets. The new wing was added by the Hays in 1575 and
subsequent additions include 17th-, 18th- and 19th-century
extensions and alterations. The crowning glory of Megginch, is,
however, the gardens. The kitchen gardens and the rose walk
(where the Jacobite rose, the white rose of York and the red rose
of Lancaster flowered together) were laid out by the Hays in the
16th century. Over the years the Drummonds filled the gardens
with exotic trees and flowers, many either collected by
themselves on their travels or imported especially from distant
lands. In 1840 the intricate flowerbeds and topiary were created.
One Drummond lady was said to 'scatter seeds wherever she
went' and the grounds and woods are certainly a mass of
flowers, including such rarities as the lovely pink violet.

❈ MENSTRIE CASTLE ❈

*T*he birthplace of Sir William Alexander of Menstrie, Earl of Stirling and, more curiously, Viscount of Canada, whose little-known and almost accidental role in the colonization of that country is one of history's more bizarre footnotes.

HISTORY

Menstrie was built in the late 16th century by a Highland family, Chiefs of the Clan McAllister, who later anglicized their name to Alexander. Close and confidential supporters of the Campbells, the Alexanders quickly grew wealthy and influential, and William, born in 1572, was to become the wealthiest and most influential of them all. An abortive love affair with a socially unacceptable local girl inspired William to write and publish over 100 sonnets dedicated to her; his poetic endeavours (and his love for falconry) brought him to the attention of James VI, who loved both. Knighted in 1609 and made 'Master of Requests' in 1614, the king went on to grant him the entire province of Nova Scotia (New Scotland), ignoring the fact that the province was already a French colony! Ever resourceful, William devised an ambitious colonization scheme which came to fruition under the next king, Charles I. The scheme, briefly, involved the payment of a large fee to the king 'by knights and gentlemen of cheife respect' in return for 16,000 acres of Nova Scotia, plus an hereditary baronetcy. The scheme was sufficiently successful for the king to reward William by making him,

successively, Secretary of State for Scotland, Viscount of Stirling, Earl of Stirling and, finally, Viscount of Canada.

FEATURES

The castle itself is an L-shaped fortified house (formerly with a courtyard), dating from the late 16th century. By the late 20th century the castle had fallen into serious disrepair and was rescued and restored by Clackmannan County Council, with the support of the National Trust for Scotland and other bodies, including the Province of Nova Scotia. It has been converted into flats and is not open to the public, with the exception of the Nova Scotia Room, which displays the 109 shields of the existing Nova Scotia baronetcies, the heraldic devices of Scotland and Nova Scotia and other coats of arms, together with portraits of King James and King Charles. The plaster ceiling motifs show the thistle and the maple leaf.

❈ MORTON CASTLE ❈

THORNHILL, DUMFRIES & GALLOWAY

*R*emote and solitary on its steep promontory, the striking ruins of Morton still tower impressively over the impenetrable waters of Castle Loch.

HISTORY

Little is known of Morton's history, for records are virtually non-existent, although it is thought that a castle stood on this site many years before Morton was built, said to have been the stronghold of Dunegal, the Lord of Nithsdale. Dunegal's grandson was Sheriff of Nithsdale in the early 13th century and he, or his son, may have been the builder of the present castle (though see below). It later passed through several hands, including on several occasions those of the Douglas Earls of Morton, and was abandoned in the early 18th century.

FEATURES

There is a considerable difference of opinion about the date of construction of this castle – estimates range from the mid-13th century to the late 15th century! The reason for this is partly due to the lack of records but also because Morton is a very unusual design for the 13-15th centuries, especially in Scotland, where the fortified house was considered to be essential. Morton is, in fact, mainly residential rather than defensive in nature and was built with considerable emphasis on comfort and aesthetic appeal. The small gatehouse, for example, though defended by two towers, drawbridge, iron yett (gate) and additional folding gates, would not have withstood an attack of any considerable force and the ground floor has as many as nine windows! The castle is only two storeys high with the ground floor containing the kitchen and other domestic offices and the first floor occupied by the spacious great hall, lit by four double, mullioned windows.

✖ MUCHALLS CASTLE ✖

A particularly fine and well-preserved example of a 17th-century laird's house.

HISTORY

Once owned by the Fraser family, the property came into the hands of the Burnets (originally Norman, de Burnard) in the early 17th century. The present house, as clearly indicated in a carving over the courtyard gateway, was begun 'be Ar. Burnet of Leys 1619. Ended be Sir Thomas Burnet of Leyis, his sonne, 1627'. The castle is extremely well preserved and is little altered externally from that time. It seems, in fact, to have had a relatively uneventful history and has certainly been left unharmed by the more extreme political and religious conflicts of the 17th and 18th centuries.

FEATURES

Muchalls Castle is more of a fortified house than a conventional castle. Built, roughly, on an E-plan, itself a development of the earlier L-plan castle, the long, main block has wings projecting at either end, with a curtain wall completing the square. The wall is well provided with gunloops and there is a triple set either side of the gateway. Crenellated open bartizans appear along the gateway wall, with a parapet in between; this was probably also crenellated and had a parapet walk at one time. The corners of the main gables carry angle turrets and there is a gabled watchroom. Such defensive features were certainly still necessary at the time Muchalls was built, but there is, too, an

overall mood of refinement and grace in the architecture, a civilizing influence which lifts any impression of the building as simply a fortress and enhances its air of elegance and taste. Internally there is some exquisite ceiling plasterwork, particularly that in the great hall which is adorned with achievements of arms, classical and biblical figures. The fireplace here has a splendid overmantel showing the Scottish royal arms and the date, 1624. Hidden within the fireplace is the opening of a narrow shaft which connects directly to a similar opening in the laird's room. This ingenious invention is a 17th-century 'bugging' device, crudely, if accurately, known as a 'laird's lug'. A rather larger shaft, in fact a smugglers' tunnel, once led from Gin Shore a mile away to the castle, but was sealed up by a later resident, a Lord Justice General of Scotland, whose lofty position made him rather sensitive to the implications of retaining such a feature in his home!

✕ MUNESS CASTLE ✕

UNST, SHETLAND ISLES

A bleak and ruinous outpost dominating an equally bleak and lonely landscape, Muness is the most northerly of all British castles.

HISTORY

Muness was built in 1598 by Laurence Bruce, a half-brother of Robert, Earl of Orkney. Bruce had been implicated in a murder which took place in his native Perthshire and he needed a refuge as far away as possible from both justice and retribution. However, Bruce seems to have become quite attached to his remote fastness as the inscription above the door testifies: this names the builder (himself) and, in rhyming verse, appeals to his offspring and heirs always 'to help and not to hurt' the structure. It appears that Bruce continued building Muness until his death, because it was finally completed by his son, Andrew. Later members of the family were not quite so attached to the castle, however, for it was abandoned within a century of its completion, after which it was burned, possibly by French pirates.

FEATURES

Bruce clearly feared that the forces of retribution might even penetrate as far north as Unst, for Muness is extremely strongly built and the walls are plentifully supplied with shotholes and gunloops. The castle is three storeys high and designed on a Z-plan, with two round towers diagonally opposite each other –

thus enabling defenders to cover both sides of the builting whilst remaining safe themselves. Not all Muness's features are purely functional, however, and the towers, shotholes and gunloops are attractively decorated. Inside, the accommodation is spacious, as befits a laird with Bruce's connections and the kitchen, with its stone sink, drain and fireplace, can still be seen.

✖ NEIDPATH CASTLE ✖

PEEBLES, BORDERS

Standing proudly amongst woods and fields in an elevated position close to the River Tweed, Neidpath Castle has silently observed 500 years of history slowly unfold around it.

HISTORY

Once owned by the powerful Norman family, the Frasers (from the French *fraise*, strawberry), the Lands of Neidpath passed through marriage to the Hay family, also of Norman origin. It was Sir William Hay who built the present tower in the early 15th century. Inevitably, perhaps, Neidpath was caught up in the political problems of the 17th century and, in 1645, was garrisoned against the forces of the Marquis of Montrose, fighting for King Charles I during the Civil Wars. In 1650 the castle was again garrisoned and besieged, but this time it was in opposition to Cromwell's Parliamentary forces. The Duke of Queensberry purchased the estate in 1686 and it has stayed in the hands of the same family until the present day.

FEATURES

The earliest part of the building, a massive, unadorned tower house, dating from the 15th century, was built primarily for defensive purposes. The walls, for example, are over 10 feet thick in places, designed to withstand bombardment by the mighty siege machines which predated cannon. In the late 17th century the castle underwent alterations and improvements which converted it from a gaunt and forbidding fortress into a

comfortable, 17th-century mansion. Aesthetic considerations now assume more prominence: the four corner lookouts, for instance, were roofed over, with the sentry walks further converted into a balustraded balcony. A series of improvements in the grounds included the planting of an avenue of trees along the approach to the castle and a fine Renaissance-style arched gateway, embellished with Fraser strawberries and the goatshead crest of the Hays.

❈ NEWARK CASTLE ❈

Nearly hidden by the now almost redundant shipyards of Port Glasgow, stubborn little Newark still retains all the proud dig-nity of its Maxwell owners.

HISTORY

The barony of Newark came into the possession of the Maxwell family in the early 15th century and shortly afterwards the family began to construct the square towerhouse; the gatehouse block and the main block were added in the mid and late 16th century. For 300 years the Maxwells seem to have enjoyed a relatively untroubled life in their castle beside the River Clyde until Sir Patrick Maxwell sold the lands around the castle to the Glasgow authorities in the late 17th century, after which the castle was soon abandoned as a residence. It is now in the care of the state.

FEATURES

Newark is now, fortunately, in an extremely good state of repair and is generally agreed to be one of the finest fortified baronial mansions still surviving in Scotland. The buildings occupy three sides of a courtyard, the fourth side being a curtain wall. Patrick Maxwell's late 16th-century additions are notable for their Renaissance detailing on the doors, windows and fireplace of the hall; this 'new' style happily cohabits with older Scots baro-

nial features such as angle turrets, gunloops, crow-stepped gables, corbelling and so on, making Newark an interesting illustration of the transitional phase between the two predominant architectural styles. The status of the Maxwells is evident in their interest in the aesthetic appeal of their home and their knowledge of current artistic movements, as well as in the airy, well-lit accommodation of the castle. The seven large Renaissance windows which light the great hall and the large fireplace with its beautiful carvings, are particularly remarkable.

❈ NIDDRY CASTLE ❈

WINCHBURGH, LOTHIAN

Still standing tall and proud on its rocky crag, this 16th-century tower house is a familiar landmark to the thousands who travel by rail between Glasgow and Edinburgh.

HISTORY

Niddry is a substantial tower house, some 500 years old, but occupied for less than half of that time. Erected by George, the 4th Lord Seton, around 1500, it lay uncompleted when he was killed, with his king, at the battle of Flodden in 1513. The 5th Lord Seton, a supporter of Mary, Queen of Scots, brought her to Niddry after her daring escape in 1568 from the Douglas stronghold at Loch Leven Castle. According to legend, Mary was so anxious to greet her people as a free woman that she came out, early next morning, with her long hair still flowing down her back. Her triumph was not destined to last long, however; 13 days later the remnants of her supporters were defeated at Langside and Mary fled to England to throw herself on the mercy of her fellow monarch, Queen Elizabeth I. Nineteen years later she was beheaded. Niddry Castle passed to the Hopes of Hopetoun in the time of Charles I, but was abandoned within a century. The castle has recently undergone extensive restoration.

FEATURES

Niddry is an early 16th-century L-shaped tower house with four storeys and a parapet. During the 17th century it evidently became necessary to increase the accommodation and, instead of

extending the walls, the owner took the unconventional step of building two additional storeys on top of the parapet. The windows of this extension were decorated with unusual pointed and arched pediments. The doorway is at ground level and opens into a guardroom; access to all floors is by a turnpike stair in the wall.

⚜ NOLTLAND CASTLE ⚜

WESTRAY, ORKNEY ISLANDS

The extensive ruins of this highly-fortified castle are an astonishing discovery on the remote island of Westray.

HISTORY

The earliest parts of Noltland date back to the 15th century, although the present structure is generally held to be the 16th-century work of Sir Gilbert Balfour, younger son of Balfour of Mountquhannie. Sir Gilbert probably acquired the property in Westray through the good offices of his brother-in-law, Adam, Bishop of the Orkneys, who, in the years following the Reformation, had much former church property to dispose of. Sir Gilbert appears to have been an unscrupulous man, closely involved in various political intrigues and feuds, including the murders of Cardinal Beaton (see St Andrews Castle), and Mary, Queen of Scots' husband, Lord Darnley. Sir Gilbert was Mary's Master of the Household and Noltland was seriously considered as a place of refuge for Mary after her escape from captivity in 1568 (see Loch Leven Castle). In 1650 Noltland was occupied as a refuge by a small group of officers from the defeated Duke of Montrose's army; the castle was soon taken by local Covenanters and, reputedly, burnt. It is now in state care.

FEATURES

This brief insight into Sir Gilbert's life and times perhaps goes some way to explain why such a surprisingly large and

well-fortified castle should be found in a comparatively remote situation. Clearly Sir Gilbert felt very insecure, for he equipped his fortress with no less than 71 gunloops, seven-foot-thick walls, corbelled parapets and turrets. The castle followed the Z-plan design and the main tower originally rose to four storeys, flanked by two strong, square towers. The main access was through an arched gateway into the courtyard and the castle door was protected by gunloops. The spacious great hall, 62 feet long and 24 feet wide, has an attractive moulded fireplace and stone seats. A smaller, private room for the laird and his family leads off the great hall and is supplied with external drains and stone seats.

⚜ RAVENSCRAIG CASTLE ⚜

KIRKCALDY, FIFE

One of the first great castles to be specifically designed for use in the 'age of artillery', Ravenscraig remains today what it always has been: a proud and imposing fortress, unembellished and unadorned, guarding the Firth of Forth from its rocky fastness.

HISTORY

When James II chose the site for the building of Ravenscraig (for his wife, Mary of Gueldres, in 1460), he could hardly have wished for anywhere more invincible than this rocky promontory with its sheer sides stretching out into the Firth of Forth, and thus guarding the sea approaches to Fife and the Lothians. James, who loved guns and was very knowledgeable about artillery, insisted that the castle be designed to withstand and return cannon fire. Ironically the king himself was killed by a cannon (named the 'Lion') which, having been over-enthusiastically stacked with gunpowder, exploded in his face. His successor, James III, compelled the Earl of Orkney to accept Ravenscraig in exchange for the Earl's Kirkwall Castle which James wanted for himself after his marriage to Margaret of Denmark. In 1651 Cromwell's General Monck, recognizing the potential danger of such a fortress should it fall into the hands of his master's enemies, ordered the castle to be dismantled, but this was done only partially.

Undoubtedly Ravenscraig's most striking feature (apart from its situation) is the provision of two very similar tower houses in one castle. In addition, the eastern tower is much lower than the western, as it necessarily accommodates the falling away of the ground near the cliff edge. The walls in these towers are 14 feet thick and there are no windows on the landward side. The towers were linked by a range topped by an artillery platform. Gunloops and gun platforms proliferate throughout the castle and the door to the beach in the eastern tower is strongly defended by two gunloops set in a wall carried on three rows of corbels.

❧ ROTHESAY CASTLE ❧

Isle of Bute, Strathclyde

$\mathcal{A}$ mighty stronghold and royal residence much fought over by kings and once captured by the Norsemen.

History

The mighty walls of Rothesay were already built when Uspak, leader of the Norsemen, attacked the castle in 1230. Unable to storm the 20 foot-high walls, Uspak's men breached them by hacking through the stone with their axes – a story borne out by a section of the wall which still shows signs of destruction and rebuilding. King Haakon himself later took control of the island but after his defeat at the great battle of Largs in 1263, Alexander III claimed the territory for Scotland. The castle was a favourite Stuart residence and was used by James IV and James V as a base from which they set forth to assert their authority over the rebellious Lords of the Isles. During the 17th-century Civil Wars, Rothesay changed hands twice – being held both for King Charles and for Cromwell. Cromwell's men partially dismantled the castle on leaving and what remained was burnt to the ground by the Duke of Argyll's followers in the 1685 Rebellion. The Marquesses of Bute undertook repairs in the 19th century; it is now in the care of the state.

Features

Even today, in its ruinous state, the castle is still awesomely impressive, with its great circular curtain walls, strengthened by

four huge round towers, the whole protected by a water-filled moat. Sharp-sighted visitors should look for the puttlog holes high up in the walls – these were designed to hold the bretache or projecting wooden enclosure which was used by the defenders to see what the attackers were doing at the base of the walls. The L-plan gatehouse tower, built by James IV and James V is a substantial structure and contains the great hall (49 feet by 25 feet) with its grand fireplace and partition to allow the laird some privacy; the upper floors are supplied with lavatory chutes to the moat. The courtyard is, uniquely in Scotland, round in shape and contains the remains of St Michael's Chapel and the well. Behind the chapel is the Bloody Stair, on which the daughter of the castle's steward stabbed herself to death to escape an arranged marriage.

⚜ ROUGH CASTLE ⚜

BONNYBRIDGE, CENTRAL

The most interesting and best-preserved of the Roman forts along the Antonine Wall.

HISTORY

The decision to abandon the further construction of Hadrian's Wall across northern England and to take the frontier line further north into Scotland was made by the Emperor Antoninus Pius, who passed the instruction to a new governor of Britain, Quintus Lollius Urbicus. The financial and military commitments to the project were considerable and involved three complete legions, a substantial proportion of Rome's regular army. Unlike Hadrian's Wall, the Antonine Wall was constructed on a rampart of turf on a stone base (approximately 14 feet wide) and stood about 10 feet high, with a ditch to the north and a military road to the south. Forts, of which Rough Castle is an excellent example, were erected approximately every two miles and were intended to house several thousand auxiliaries. The wall was finally abandoned by the Romans in 163 AD.

FEATURES

Although there is little of the original fort to be seen, excavations and restoration work show a section of the Antonine Wall and the earthworks spread over an area of about one acre which make up the fort. The fort is protected by the rampart of the road, its main gate (facing north) forming part of

the wall itself. Thus a patrol or a defensive force could rapidly emerge from the fort, cross the ditch over a mound and, carefully avoiding the 10 rows of pits containing sharpened stakes, repel the attackers. On the south side of the wall the hard-topped military road (about 18 feet wide) runs through the fort. The sites of the headquarters building, commander's house and granary, all stone built, have been located as well as a timber barracks. An annexe on the eastern side contained the bathhouse. The wall formed a shield for the fort on one side with the remaining three sides being protected by ditches.

✵ ST ANDREWS CASTLE ✵

St Andrews, Fife

$\mathcal{A}$lthough largely ruinous, once-powerful St Andrews is still notable for its impressive situation, on a rocky headland jutting into the North Sea, and for its rich historical associations.

HISTORY

The first castle at St Andrews was built by Bishop Roger in around 1200; the community of St Andrews was fast developing into a religious centre and the castle served as the Bishop's Palace. The troubled period between 1330 and 1385 saw the castle destroyed, rebuilt and destroyed again until Walter Traill became bishop and constructed another new building. The most notorious event associated with the castle was the execution in March 1546 of George Wishart, an active participant in the Protestant Scottish Reformation movement. Wishart was burnt at the stake in front of the castle at the behest of the then resident, Cardinal Beaton, who viewed the scene from the castle walls. Beaton's triumph was short-lived, however, since he himself was taken prisoner by a group of Protestant Reformers (who, ironically, managed to gain access to the castle by joining a party of masons undertaking work for the cardinal to strengthen the castle's defences). Beaton was duly murdered in revenge for Wishart's death and his body was hung over the battlements. The Protestants then took control of the castle and held it for over a year, provisioned by the English from the sea. It was only when a French fleet, sent to help the Roman Catholic party in Scotland, cut off English aid that the defenders surrendered in 1547. The Reformers (including John Knox) were taken prisoner and deported by the French. The abolition of episcopacy in Scotland in 1560 brought the castle's function to an end, and in 1654 much of the stone was used to repair the town harbour. The castle was ruinous by the late 17th century and in 1801 several buildings on the eastern side fell into the sea.

FEATURES

Although the remains of St Andrews are scant, the bottle dungeon (cut out of the rock) still survives, as do the underground tunnels (now floodlit) dug by both defenders and attackers in 1547.

�֎ SKIPNESS CASTLE ✖

SKIPNESS, STRATHCLYDE

Commanding unsurpassed views across Kilbrannan Sound to the
ragged peaks of Arran, ruined Skipness was once an important
and strategic stronghold in the struggles for clan supremacy.

HISTORY

Although accurate details of the castle's history are extremely
scarce, it is known to have been a much-coveted prize in the
local conflicts for clan power and control and was occupied,
variously, by MacSweens, Macdonalds, Stewarts and
Campbells (it once marked the boundary of the Campbell
lands), and dates, probably, from the 13th century. Skipness
Castle's mighty walls (up to eight feet thick) and strong tower
(mainly 16th century) indicate its strategic importance. In the
17th century the castle came into the hands of the Campbell
Earls of Argyll and the king ordered its destruction after the
Argyll Rising of 1685, although this order was never carried
out. Skipness was last occupied in the 17th century and later
converted into a farm; the farm buildings were removed many
years ago and the castle was later taken into state care. An
extensive repair programme is under way.

FEATURES

The castle compound consists of a quadrangular curtain wall
incorporating a four storey tower house at one corner, topped
by a gabled caphouse, parapet walks and four open turrets.
The tower house is a reconstruction of the earlier 13th-century

tower, and this is particularly evident in the basement, where the walls incorporate those of the earlier castle. A projecting turret fulfils a dual purpose – it contains drains with wide outside chutes for refuse and gunloops for defence. The main access was originally on the seaward side and

the castle must have seemed a most awesome sight to those approaching in a small boat, with its embattled keep, massive walls and soaring towers.

❈ SMAILHOLM TOWER ❈

SMAILHOLM, BORDERS

Smailholm is one of the finest examples of a Borders peel tower still to be seen.

HISTORY

For centuries the Borders region was notorious for the wild and lawless behaviour of its inhabitants, particularly the violent and murderous activities of the 'reivers' or raiders. One family of prosperous Borders farmers, the Pringles, decided, sometime in the 16th century, to build themselves a strong, defensive (peel) tower to provide greater security for their people and portable property. Plain and unadorned, Smailholm has no pretensions towards grandeur, but would have been a safe refuge and watchtower from which they could observe the approaching bands of horsemen. Few details are known of Smailholm's subsequent history, although it is known to have been sold to the Scotts in the 17th century. The family built a new house nearby (to which the novelist, Sir Walter Scott, was a frequent visitor; he found Smailholm a great inspiration), and soon abandoned the tower as a residence. It is now in state care.

FEATURES

Smailholm Tower sits on the remote and isolated Sandyknowe Crags, protected on three sides by rocks and on the fourth by water. Possibly the finest extant example of a peel tower, its stern practicality is its most notable feature. The whinstone walls, for example, are almost 6 feet thick and the few windows (protected by iron grilles) are well above ground level. The single entrance is guarded by a strong iron yett (gate) with gunport overhead. The tower rises to four storeys and has parapet walks on two sides of the top floor commanding outstanding views across the countryside; the north parapet wall has a small shelter beside the chimney for the watchman and a recess for his lantern. Internally, the

tower follows the usual 16th-century pattern with a great hall above the vaulted basement and the family's private rooms on the top two storeys. The tower was originally surrounded by a courtyard containing other domestic buildings and an enclosing wall (barmkin); these have recently been excavated and studied.

❈ SPYNIE CASTLE ❈

SPYNIE, ELGIN, GRAMPIAN

The great ruined palace of the once-powerful Bishops of Moray, this is the most splendid bishop's palace in the country.

HISTORY

Although the cathedral, originally at Spynie, was rebuilt in Elgin during the 13th century, the Bishops of Moray continued to live at Spynie and the palace is noted in the survey made for Edward I during his invasion of Scotland in the late 13th century. The account states that it was well defended with thick walls, watchtower and portcullis, and protected by a moat. Such fortifications for a bishop's palace may seem at odds with the Christian role assigned to him, but powerful churchmen of this period had to be at least as martial and uncompromising as the members of their congregations. For example, in the 15th century, in response to threats from the Earl of Huntly, whom he had excommunicated, Bishop David Stewart (died 1476) built Spynie's great tower, one of the largest of its kind in Scotland. Mary, Queen of Scots stayed briefly at the palace in 1562 and it played a prominent role in the religious troubles of the 17th century, being held by both Royalists and Covenanters. The palace became Crown property in 1690, after which it was soon abandoned and used as a quarry. It is now in the care of the state and an extensive programme of repairs will soon be completed.

FEATURES

The 15th-century David's Tower, though ruined, dominates the palace and is a potent reminder of the defensive role the Church was forced to play to protect itself against its aggressive flock. This mighty structure rises six storeys high, its walls are up to ten feet thick and it was originally crowned by a parapet, open turrets and caphouse. To improve its defence, the main entrance was on the first floor and access was by a movable drawbridge. The bishops did, of course, live in some considerable splendour and the great hall, hung with colourful tapestries, warmed by a blazing fire and with soft cushions on the windowseats, would have been a fine room.

※ STIRLING CASTLE ※

STIRLING, CENTRAL

The 'Key to Scotland', Stirling links the North and South and has changed hands more often than any other stronghold in the country.

HISTORY

Like Edinburgh Castle, Stirling sits high on volcanic rock although here the site is more open and the castle is visible for miles around, despite the encroachment of suburbia. As a fortress of vital strategic importance, the castle's own history is deeply enmeshed with the major events of the history of the nation. Stirling assumed a prominent role in the Wars of Independence, for example, as it guarded the routes northwards. Initially the English took the castle easily, but in 1304, with Stirling once more in Scottish hands, Edward I mounted a great siege against the castle, the last one to be still under the control of the Scottish patriots. The siege lasted three months until the defenders were forced to surrender by starvation. For 10 years Stirling was then manned by an English garrison until, in 1314, besieged by the Scots, the English troops sent to relieve it suffered a devastating defeat at Bannockburn nearby. By the mid-14th century the castle was firmly back under Scottish control and, during the reigns of the Scottish monarchs, it assumed a more peaceful role as a favoured royal residence, seeing its share of feasting, dancing and tournaments. (There were, however, some darker deeds perpetrated within its walls during this period, such as the murder of William, the 8th Earl of Douglas,

by James II, who compounded the crime by having the victim's body unceremoniously tossed out of a nearby window! See Threave Castle.) James III was born at Stirling and James IV visited the castle frequently as he much enjoyed hunting in the surrounding forests; James V, a humane and cultured man, stayed at the castle as a child and with his second wife, Mary of Guise. James VI was baptised in the Old Chapel, which he had completely rebuilt for the baptism of his own son in 1594. (The overall cost of the baptism of Prince Frederick Henry James was £100,000!)

The Union of the Crowns in 1603 meant that Stirling's importance as a strategic stronghold and royal residence was largely diminished and it came to be used mainly to house distinguished prisoners, although during the Civil Wars it was besieged and taken by General Monck on behalf of Cromwell after only a few days; this was not due to any weakness of the castle but because of a mutiny amongst the soldiers of the garrison. The castle was from then on held by the Crown and it played a significant role in the 1715 and 1745 Risings by holding out against the Highlanders. After 1745 Stirling continued as a barracks and eventually became the headquarters of the Argyll and Sutherland Highlanders. In 1964 the army left and the long, slow process of restoration, already begun at the turn of the century, accelerated.

FEATURES

Although there have been fortifications here since the early 12th century, little of what we see today dates from before the 15th century. The outer defences, approached over a wide ditch, were constructed in the 18th century; the arched entrance in the curtain wall bears the monogram of Queen Anne. Inside there is a further defensive rampart, including a gatehouse and, beyond, the residential buildings including James III's great hall, James V's palace and James VI's chapel. The great hall has, unfortunately, been much altered since its construction when it had five magnificent fireplaces (storage space for wood and coal was provided under the floor), and an impressive hammer-beam roof. The windows were placed high up to allow for tapestries to be fully displayed on the walls. The palace, built under the supervision of the notorious James Hamilton of Finnart, the King's Master of Works (see Craignethan Castle), was designed in Renaissance style – one of the first in Scotland to incorporate extensive use of classic Renaissance details. The series of recessed ornamental panels is typical of this movement and the varied collection of sculptures – which includes gods, the Devil and the king himself – are particularly entertaining. The palace rooms encircle an open court known, perfectly accurately, as the Lion's Den – for it housed the royal lion. James VI's chapel is early Renaissance style and remains largely unaltered, except for the removal of royal coats of arms and crests by Cromwell's men.

❋ TANTALLON CASTLE ❋

North Berwick, Lothian

A mighty ruined stronghold on a rugged clifftop, rose-red Tantallon was the fortress of the powerful and rebellious 'Red Douglas' family.

History

The history of the 'Red Douglas' clan, Earls of Angus, is one of so many deceits, betrayals, intrigues, rebellions, sieges and exiles that it almost defies belief. One Earl of Angus, for example, found himself so out of favour with his king, James IV, in 1491 that he was besieged at Tantallon by the monarch himself; by the next year, however, this same man was created Chancellor of Scotland! The 6th Earl married James IV's widow, Queen Margaret, but was suspected of treasonably plotting to overthrow the Scottish king in favour of Henry VIII in 1528. Again Tantallon was besieged but after 20 days the king abandoned the attack and the Earl, who had meanwhile escaped, returned in triumph. His triumph was to be short-lived, however, as Angus was exiled in 1529 and the king took control of the castle for the next 14 years. James V's death in 1542 allowed Angus to return. By 1543 England and Scotland were at war. Angus changed sides twice in the ensuing years, irritating Henry so much that he offered 2000 crowns for the treacherous Earl's head! When Angus finally died (of natural causes) at Tantallon in 1556, his successor fully lived up to the family traditions by being twice exiled for treachery. A later Earl was also exiled – but this time for changing his religious allegiances twice! The

castle was attacked by Cromwell's General Monck in 1651, in 1699 it was sold and shortly afterwards abandoned.

FEATURES

This brief glance at the history of the Earls of Angus suggests that they certainly needed a really substantial fortress as a base, and Tantallon, one of the most impressive castles in Scotland, certainly fulfils this criterion. Protected by the sea on two sides, with earthworks and a deep ditch on the other, it would appear to be almost impregnable. The castle is built round a quadrangle and dates from the end of the 14th century. The mighty curtain wall, 12 feet thick and 50 feet high, is strengthened by two towers and a gatehouse, 80 feet high and with four storeys of living accommodation. Tantallon's reputation was fearsome.

⚜ THIRLESTANE CASTLE ⚜

LAUDER, BORDERS

Beginning its life as a plain unadorned fortress, Thirlestane was transformed into a castle and then into a true palace.

HISTORY

It was Sir John Maitland, James VI's faithful chancellor, who first began the transformation of Thirlestane by enlarging and modernizing the old fort of Lauder in the late 16th century. Maitland's heir, the Duke of Lauderdale, had much grander ideas, however, and, together with his wife, Elizabeth Murray, was determined to create a showpiece that would dazzle everyone with the visible evidence of their power, influence and wealth. The architect, William Bruce, adapted Maitland's simpler design into an innovative mixture of classical and baronial styles. For the interiors Lauderdale employed the king's favourite craftsmen, dishonestly diverting to Thirlestane both the men from their official labours at Edinburgh Castle as well as the public funds with which he paid for the work. Nevertheless, the plasterers created an astonishingly extravagant set of stateroom ceilings for the castle, unequalled in the country. When, finally, Thirlestane was complete and furnished it had become a lavish, if occasionally vulgar, display of wealth and power which was exactly what its owners intended it to be. When the duke died, however, his widow virtually abandoned the castle, moving 14 wagonloads of furniture to her southern home, much to the outrage of the local people. Thirlestane is now owned and managed by a charitable trust with the

Maitland-Carew family retaining their links by occupying a wing of the castle.

FEATURES

William Bruce took the old tower as the core of his 17th-century alterations, but created a new entrance with a flight of stairs, a classical doorway and a balcony, crowned with a large ogee-roofed central feature. Other mock-Scots baronial details were added in the 19th century. Internally the old tower arrangement of interconnecting rooms remains the same, but the increasingly elaborate ceilings are breathtaking in their virtuosity. The fine panelling and swan pediments over the doors were worked by Dutch craftsmen.

❈ THREAVE CASTLE ❈

THREAVE, DUMFRIES & GALLOWAY

The seat and home of the fearsome and notorious 'Black Douglas' family, Lords of Galloway, whose ambition rivalled even that of the Stewart kings themselves.

HISTORY

The stronghold of the 3rd Earl of Douglas, Archibald 'the Grim', Threave was constructed in the late 14th century, and it was from here that the two young Douglas heirs rode away to Edinburgh Castle and their deaths at the famous Black Dinner of 1440. This crude attempt by the Regents Livingstone and Crichton to curb the power of the Douglases during the minority of James II was echoed by the king himself when, 12 years later, he himself stabbed and fatally wounded the 8th Earl (see Stirling Castle). Inevitably, perhaps, given their lawless ways, the Douglases themselves gave James II the excuse he needed to launch a final attack on the family, and this came when the Douglas laird hanged Sir Patrick MacLellan of Bombie, against the king's express orders. The king marched against the Douglas strongholds until there was only Threave left. James himself commanded the siege against the castle. By this time Earl James was far away in safety (in England) and the garrison suddenly capitulated (bribery is often cited as the reason for the suddenness of the surrender). Thereafter Threave became a royal fortress and, in the 17th century, was besieged and captured by Covenanters (those who opposed the king's religious policies), who left it severely damaged – although it

was evidently considered good enough to house French prisoners of war taken in the Napoleonic Wars over 150 years later!

FEATURES

The massive walls, 70 feet high and 8 feet thick, are all that now remain of Archibald's 14th-century castle (the outer wall and four round towers, only one of which still survives, were built the following century when it became a royal castle). Access to the castle was then, as now, by boat which docked at a movable wooden bridge leading to the door. Of particular interest are the puttlog holes in the walls, used for fixing the bretache (or covered wooden platform projecting over the walls so that defenders could see what was happening at the vulnerable base of the castle walls), and the granite projection, known as the Gallow's Knob, from which Douglas enemies were hanged; it was never, remarked Archibald the Grim, 'without a tassel'.

❈ TOLQUHON CASTLE ❈

TARVES, GRAMPIAN

A fine Scots baronial castle and a vivid illustration of the development of Scottish domestic architecture between the 15th and 16th centuries.

HISTORY

Sir John Forbes acquired Tolquhon on his marriage to a Preston heiress, Marjorie, in 1420, and soon after began to build a sturdy tower. By 1584 the family was prosperous enough for the laird, William Forbes, a cultured and civilized man, to enlarge and alter his home in line with the more enlightened and progressive developments of late 16th-century domestic architecture. William was so pleased with the result that he set down his achievement in stone, carved above the entrance so that all posterity might know that he was responsible for it: 'All this wark, except the Auld Tour, was begun be William Forbes 15 April 1584, and endit be him 20 October 1589.' The family went from strength to strength – even acquiring a knighthood in 1651, awarded to Alexander, the 10th laird, by Charles II, whose life he had saved at the battle of Worcester. Thereafter, however, Alexander's mishandling of the family fortunes led to severe financial difficulties and the estate had to be sold in 1716. The Forbes were a tenacious family, however, and it was to be two years before William, the 11th laird, was forcibly escorted from Tolquhon by a party of soldiers.

FEATURES

Situated on rising ground, dotted with fine old yew trees, Tolquhon, though ruined, remains an impressive and distinctive structure, successfully bringing together the pragmatic (the necessary defensive features) with the pleasing (decorative details and so on). Beyond the unusually large outer courtyard, for example, is the great gatehouse, flanked by two formidable drum (round) towers, complete with guardrooms and heavily barred windows. The gunloops, however, are decorated and the gatehouse itself is embellished with carved armorial designs and Renaissance style sculpture. Through the gatehouse lies a gracious mansion with a central courtyard. The buildings are carefully planned for domestic use and, whilst they are well supplied with gunloops and barred windows, several courtyard windows are unusually large for the period.

⚜ URQUHART CASTLE ⚜

Drumnadrochit, Highland

The battered remains of Urquhart, once one of the largest and most strategically important castles in Scotland, still stand silent guard over the mysterious waters of world-famous Loch Ness.

History

Originally standing 50 feet above water level (the loch was raised 6 feet when the Caledonian Canal was built), Urquhart Castle was a stronghold of immense political significance, commanding panoramic views of Loch Ness, a vitally important communications route and part of the Great Glen. Because of its key strategic importance, Urquhart's history is dominated by capture, destruction and rebuilding. The present remains were built by Alan Durward, Justiciar of Scotland, in the mid-13th century. In 1296 Urquhart was garrisoned by Edward I of England, who was forced to recapture it later after a long siege (1303). English success was short-lived, however, and within a few years Urquhart was once again in Scottish hands — where it remained for many years in spite of Edward III's efforts to recapture it. In the 16th century Urquhart was attacked and pillaged several times by the wild and restless Macdonalds, in spite of the best efforts of John Grant of Freuchie, who had been given Urquhart by James IV on condition that he made specific improvements and kept it in good repair. In 1644 a roaming band of Covenanters ransacked the castle and in 1689 the inhabitants fought off an attack by Jacobites. Shortly after this the castle was dismantled as a safety measure by government forces.

FEATURES

The two most complete structures of this once-powerful stronghold are the gatehouse and the 16th-century tower, which still shows the traces of its attractive and well-equipped 17th century corner turrets – each with its own fireplace, window, gunloop and toilet facilities! The views, of course, are unsurpassed and, so it is said, there have been more sightings of the Loch Ness monster from this vantage point than from anywhere else. (Sightings of the monster, incidentally, have been recorded since the 6th century!)

Ashlar: masonry with large blocks of stone squared and given a smooth face.

Astragal: (Scots) wooden glazing bar, between window panes.

Aumbry: recess or cupboard within the thickness of a wall.

Bailey: the courtyard of a castle.

Barbican: an outwork defending the entrance to a castle.

Barmkin: (Scots) enclosing wall of small courtyard, especially of towerhouse; also the small courtyard attached to a towerhouse.

Bartizan: corbelled turret, round or square, at the corners of the battlements of a castle.

Batter: a slight inward slope on wall from its base upwards.

Battlement: parapet at top of castle wall going 'up and down'; the solid section is termed a merlon and the lower section between a crenel.

Belfry: siege tower.

Bretache: a defensive wooden gallery built out from the wall head.

Cap-house: (Scots) the small room at the top of a turnpike stair, often partly corbelled out. (see also **corbel**).

Close: (Scots) a passage or courtyard giving access to several buildings.

Corbel: stone part-projecting from wall to carry roof- or floor-timber or carrying further row of projecting stones.

Corbie-step: see **crow step**.

Crenel: the lower indentations in a battlement (see also **merlon**).

Crow step: a gable at the end of a roof, the diagonal of which is stepped (see also **skew**).

Curtain wall: connecting wall between the towers of a castle.

Dais: raised platform at the end of a great hall for the high table.

Donjon: the keep of a castle or the most strongly-fortified mural tower, where the lord of the castle had his residence.

Doocot: (Scots) a dovecote.

Dormer window: a window standing up vertically from the slope of a roof; it may spring from the wallhead or from part-way up the roof.

Draw-bar slot: the recesses left to fasten the heavy wooden draw-bar, which acted as a bolt across the back of doors of gates.

Drawbridge: the end part of a bridge, or in many cases the whole bridge, which could be raised to leave a gap over the ditch.

Dressings: features such as quoins or window-surrounds made of smoothly-worked stone.

Droved ashlar: the normal surface-finish to fine stonework in medieval Scotland, with thin parallel lines, usually at a diagonal angle across the face of the stone.

Embattled: possessing battlements.

Enceinte, Castle of: (French: enclosure) castle possessing stone curtain wall and towers.

Entresol: a mezzanine storey built into the arched vault of a tall room.

Feu: (Scots) land granted by feudal superior to vassal or feuar on condition that he pays an annual feu-duty.

Freestone: stone which can be cut in all directions, so that it will take a shape.

Frieze: a horizontal band of ornament, around the top of the walls of a room.

Garderobe: a medieval latrine.

Hammer-beam: a particular type of roof-truss in late-medieval architecture, in which the main beams are supported on short cantilevered beams resting on the wall-plate.

Harling: (Scots) wet dash or roughcasting, hurled or dashed on to a wall to protect against the weather.

Hoarding: see **bretache**.

Jamb: (Scots) A wing or extension adjoining one side of the main block of, say, a towerhouse.

245

Joist: beam supporting floor.

Laird: (Scots) a landowner (literally, a lord).

Lancet: a single-light window with a sharply pointed head.

Lintel: a horizontal beam of stone bridging an opening.

Machicolation: a series of openings in a stone parapet through which missiles or boiling liquid could be dropped on to attackers beneath.

Merlon: see **battlement**.

Motte: a steep mound, part of an earthwork castle.

Moulding: ornament around door, window, etc., of continuous or repeating profile.

Mullion: the vertical divider between the lights (compartments) of a window opening (see also **transom**).

Mural stair: stair ascending within the thickness of the wall and parallel to the latter's direction.

Newel: the centre post in a turnpike or spiral stairway.

Oratory: a small private domestic chapel.

Oriel: window projecting externally, with its base corbelled out .

Palisade: a wooden stockade surrounding an enclosure.

Pantile: a roof-tile of curved S-shape section.

Parapet: a low wall, sometimes battlemented, on the edge of a drop.

Pediment: a triangular gable over doors or windows.

Peel, pele: a stone towerhouse near the Scottish-English border.

Pend: (Scots) an open-ended passage through a building, at ground level.

Pit prison: a prison the only entrance to which is through a trap-door in the roof.

Pleasaunce: (Scots) a walled garden.

Plinth: the lowest courses of a wall, when these are either projecting further than the upper parts or are battered (see **batter**).

Policies: the park or grounds attached to a castle.

Portcullis: a gate sliding up and down vertical grooves or slots cut in the sides of a castle gateway.

Postern: small gateway, allowing access on foot to a castle.

Puttlog hole: holes in a wall constructed to receive cross-timbers of original wooden scaffold, and insufficiently filled in.

Quoins: dressed stones at the angles of a building.

Rampart: stone or earth wall surrounding a castle.

Re-entrant angle: the wall of a jamb which is overlooked by the main part of a towerhouse, and where the entrance is usually sited.

Relieving arch: arch set in the wall just above a lintel to divert the pressure from the centre of the lintel which might break it.

Roll-moulding: moulding of near-circular section.

Rubble: masonry, the stones of which are wholly or partially left rough.

Scale-and-platt: a stair with straight flights and intermediate landings.

Scarcement: a ledge running along a wall to support the beams for a floor.

Scarp: a steep slope.

Skew: the sloping stones on a gable with a diagonal profile (see also **crow step**).

Solar: private living room of the lord in a medieval dwelling.

String-course: projecting horizontal moulding on exterior of a building.

Transe: (Scots) passage, especially screens passage in great hall.

Transom: horizontal divider between the lights (compartments) of a window opening (see also **mullion**).

Turnpike: (Scots) a spiral stair.

Turret: a small tower attached to a building.

Vault: an arched stone ceiling.

Wainscot: wood panelling on a wall.

Yett: a door of interwoven iron bars, used to reinforce wooden doors at the entrance to towerhouses.

ABERDEENSHIRE

Balmoral Castle May-Jul., Mon.-Sat. 1000-1700.

Braemar Castle May-mid.Oct., Sat.-Thurs. 1000-1800.

Castle Fraser Easter, May-Jun. and Sep., daily 1330-1730. Jul.-Aug. daily, 1100-1730. Weekends in Oct. 1330-1730. Garden and grounds all year, daily 0930-1800 or sunset.

Craigievar Castle May-Sep., daily 1330-1730. Grounds all year, daily 0930-sunset.

Crathes Castle Easter-Oct., daily 1100-1730. Garden and grounds all year, daily 0900-sunset.

Drum Castle Easter, May-Sep., daily 1330-1730. Weekends in Oct. 1330-1730. Grounds all year, daily 0930-sunset.

Dunnottar Castle Apr.-Oct., Mon.-Sat. 0900-1730, Sun 1400-1630. Nov.-Mar., Mon.-Fri. 0900-sunset.

Fyvie Castle Easter-Jun. and Sep., daily 1330-1730. Jul.-Aug., daily 1100-1730. Weekends in Oct. 1330-1730. Grounds all year, daily 0930-sunset.

Glenbuchat Castle Open access all year.

Huntly Castle Apr.-Sep., Mon.-Sat. 0930-1830, Sun. 1400-1830. Oct.-Mar., Mon.-Sat. 0930-1630 (except closed Thur. pm and all day Fri.), Sun. 1400-1630.

Kildrummy Castle Apr.-Sep., Mon.-Sat. 0930-1830, Sun. 1400-1830.

Muchall's Castle Now run as a country house hotel.

Tolquhon Castle Apr.-Sep., Mon.-Sat. 0930-1830, Sun. 1400-1830. Oct.-Mar., Sat. 0930-1630, Sun. 1400-1630.

ANGUS

Edzell Castle Apr.-Sep., Mon.-Sat. 0930-1830, Sun. 1400-1830. Oct.-Mar., Mon.-Sat. 0930-1630 (except closed Thur. pm and all day Fri.), Sun. 1400-1630.

Glamis Castle Easter-mid. Oct., daily 1030-1730.

Carnasserie Castle Open access all year.
Castle Sween Open access all year.
Duart Castle May-Sep., daily 1030-1800.
Dunstaffnage Castle Apr.-Sep., Mon.-Sat. 0930-1830, Sun. 1400-1830.
Inveraray Castle Apr.-Jun. and Sep.-Oct., Mon.-Thur. and Sat 1000-1300 and 1400-1730, Sun. 1300-1730. Jul.-Aug., Mon.-Sat. 1000-1730, Sun. 1300-1730.
Rothesay Castle Apr.-Sep., Mon.-Sat. 0930-1830, Sun. 1400-1830. Oct.-Mar., Mon.-Sat. 0930-1630 (except closed Thur. pm and all day Fri.), Sun. 1400-1630.
Skipness Castle Apr.-Sep., open access. Contact Historic Scotland, tel. 0131 668 8800 for details of winter openings.

Ayton Castle Open summer Sunday afternoons. Tel. 018907 81212 for details.
Floors Castle Easter, May-Jun. and Sep., Sun.-Thur. 1030-1730. Jul.-Aug., Mon.-Sun. 1030-1730. Oct., Wed. and Sun. only 1030-1600.
Hermitage Castle Apr.-Sep., Mon.-Sat. 0930-1830, Sun. 1400-1830.
Neidpath Castle Easter-Oct., Mon.-Sat. 1100-1700, Sun. 1300-1500.
Smailholm Tower Apr.-Sep., Mon.-Sat. 0930-1830, Sun. 1400-1830.
Thirlestane Castle Easter, May-Jun. and Sep., Sun., Mon., Wed., Thur. 1400-1700, grounds 1200-1800. Jul.-Aug., Sun.-Fri. 1400-1700.

Craigmillar Castle Apr.-Sep., Mon.-Sat. 0930-1830, Sun. 1400-1830. Oct.-Mar., Mon.-Sat. 0930-1630 (except closed Thur. pm and all day Fri.), Sun. 1400-1630.
Edinburgh Castle Apr.-Sep., daily 0930-1715. Oct.-Mar., daily 0930-1615.

Lauriston Castle Apr.-Oct., Sat.-Thur. 1100-1300, 1400-1700. Nov.-Mar., weekends only 1400-1600. Grounds open all year, daily 0900-sunset.

CITY OF GLASGOW

Crookston Castle Key obtainable from Castle Cottage at all reasonable times.

CLACKMANNAN

Castle Campbell Apr.-Sep., Mon.-Sat. 0930-1830, Sun. 1400-1830. Oct.-Mar., Mon.-Sat. 0930-1630 (except closed Thur. pm and all day Fri.), Sun. 1400-1630.
Menstrie Castle Easter weekend, May-Sep., Sat. and Sun. only, 1400-1700. Confirm details with Stirling Tourist Information Centre, tel. 01786 475019.

DUMFRIES AND GALLOWAY

Caerlaverock Castle Apr.-Sep., Mon.-Sat. 0930-1830, Sun. 1400-1830. Oct.-Mar., Mon.-Sat. 0930-1630, Sun. 1400-1630.
Cardoness Castle Apr.-Sep., Mon.-Sat. 0930-1830, Sun. 1400-1830. Oct.-Mar., Sat. 0930-1630, Sun. 1400-1630.
Carsluith Castle Open access all year.
Comlongan Castle All year, daily 1000-1700.
Drumlanrig Castle May-Aug., Fri.-Wed. 1100-1700. Grounds Fri.-Wed., 1100-1800.
Lochmaben Castle Open access all year.
Lochnaw Castle Contact Stranraer Tourist Information Centre (Easter-Oct., tel. 01776 702595) for access information.
MacLellan's Castle Apr.-Sep., Mon.-Sat., 0930-1830, Sun. 1400-1830.
Morton Castle Open access all year.

Broughty Castle Jul.-Sep., Mon. 1100-1300, 1400-1700, Tue.-Thur. and Sat. 1000-1300, 1400-1700, Sun. 1400-1700. Contact Dundee Tourist Information Centre, tel. 01382 434664, for details of winter openings.

Claypotts Castle No access to interior. Contact Historic Scotland, tel. 0131 668 8800, for viewing information.

EAST AYRSHIRE

Loch Doon Castle Open access all year.

EAST DUNBARTONSHIRE

Dumbarton Castle Apr.-Sep., Mon.-Sat. 0930-1830, Sun. 1400-1830. Oct.-Mar., Mon.-Sat. 0930-1630 (except closed Thur. pm and all day Fri.), Sun. 1400-1630.

EAST LOTHIAN

Dirleton Castle Apr.-Sep., Mon.-Sat. 0930-1830, Sun. 1400-1830. Oct.-Mar., Mon.-Sat. 0930-1630, Sun. 1400-1630.

Dunbar Castle Open access all year.

Hailes Castle Open access all year.

Tantallon Castle Apr.-Sep., Mon.-Sat. 0930-1830, Sun. 1400-1830. Oct.-Mar., Mon.-Sat. 0930-1630 (except closed Thur. pm and all day Fri.), Sun. 1400-1630.

FALKIRK

Blackness Castle Apr.-Sep., Mon.-Sat. 0930-1830, Sun. 1400-1830. Oct.-Mar., Mon.-Sat. 0930-1630 (except closed Thur. pm and all day Fri.), Sun. 1400-1630

Rough Castle Open access all year.

Aberdour Castle Apr.-Sep., Mon.-Sat. 0930-1830, Sun. 1400-1830. Oct.-Mar., Mon.-Sat. 0930-1630 (except closed Thur. pm and all day Fri.), Sun. 1400-1630.

Balgonie Castle Open all year, daily 1000-1700. Tel. 01592 750119 for details.

Royal Palace of Falkland Easter-Oct., Mon.-Sat. 1100-1730. Sun. 1330-1730.

Kellie Castle Easter, May-Sep., daily 1330-1730. Weekends in Oct. 1330-1730. Gardens and grounds all year, daily 0930-sunset.

Ravenscraig Castle Open access to exterior all year.

St Andrew's Castle Apr.-Sep., Mon.-Sat. 0930-1830, Sun. 1400-1830. Oct.-Mar., Mon.-Sat. 0930-1630, Sun. 1400-1630.

HIGHLAND

Cawdor Castle May-Sep., daily 1000-1730.

Dunrobin Castle Easter, May and Oct., Mon.-Sat. 1030-1630, Sun. 1300-1630. Jun.-Sep., Mon.-Sat. 1030-1730, Sun. 1300-1730.

Dunvegan Castle Mid. Mar.-Oct., Mon.-Sat. 1000-1730, Sun. 1300-1700.

Eilean Donan Castle Easter-Sep., daily 1000-1800.

Girnigoe Castle Open access all year (ruins and nearby cliffs very dangerous).

Invergarry Castle The castle can be seen from the grounds of the Glengarry Castle Hotel; there is no access to the interior of the castle for safety reasons.

Urquhart Castle Apr.-Sep., daily 0930-1830. Oct.-Mar., daily 0930-1630.

INVERCLYDE

Newark Castle Apr.-Sep., Mon.-Sat. 0930-1830, Sun. 1400-1830.

Crichton Castle Apr.-Sep., Mon.-Sat. 0930-1830, Sun. 1400-1630.

MORAY

Ballindalloch Castle The castle is a family home and is open to the public Easter-Sep., daily, tel. 01807 500206 for details.

Balvenie Castle Apr.-Sep., Mon.-Sat. 0930-1830, Sun. 1400-1830.

Brodie Castle Easter-Sep., Mon.-Sat. 1100-1730, Sun. 1330-1730. Weekends in Oct., Sat. 1100-1730, Sun. 1330-1730. Grounds all year, daily 0930-sunset.

Darnaway Castle By appointment only. Write to Estates Office, Forres, Moray IV36 0ET.

Duffus Castle Open access all year.

Spynie Castle Apr.-Sep., Mon.-Sat. 0930-1830, Sun. 1400-1830. Oct.-Mar., Sat., Sun. only 1400-1630.

NORTH AYRSHIRE

Brodick Castle Easter-Oct., daily 1130-1700. Gardens and country park open all year, daily 0930-sunset,

Kelburn Castle Limited summer opening. Tel. 01475 568685/568554 for details.

Lochranza Castle Apr.-Sep., open all reasonable times.

ORKNEY

Noltland Castle Open access all year.

PERTH AND KINROSS

Blair Castle Apr.-Oct., daily 1000-1800.

Burleigh Castle Apr.-Sep., open access. Contact Historic Scotland, tel. 0131 668 8800, for details of winter opening.

Castle Menzies Apr.-mid.Oct., Mon.-Sat. 1030-1700, Sun. 1400-1700.

Elcho Castle Contact Historic Scotland, tel. 0131 668 8800, for details of opening.

Huntingtower Castle Apr.-Sep., Mon.-Sat. 0930-1830, Sun. 1400-1830. Oct.-Mar., Mon.-Sat. 0930-1630 (except closed Thur. pm and all day Fri.), Sun. 1400-1630.

Loch Leven Castle Apr.-Sep., Mon.-Sat. 0930-1830, Sun. 1400-1830.

Megginch Castle No access to the castle. Gardens open Apr.-Jun. and Sep.-Oct., Wed. only 1400-1700. Jul.-Aug., Mon.-Fri 1400-1700.

SHETLAND

Muness Castle Open access at all reasonable times.

SOUTH AYRSHIRE

Culzean Castle Easter-Oct., daily 1030-1730. Country park all year, daily 0930-sunset.

Dundonald Castle Tel. 01563 850201 for details of opening.

Threave Castle Apr.-Sep., Mon.-Sat. 0930-1830, Sun. 1400-1830 (includes a short ferry trip).

SOUTH LANARKSHIRE

Bothwell Castle Apr.-Sep., Mon.-Sat. 0930-1830, Sun. 1400-1830. Oct.-Mar., Mon.-Sat. 0930-1630 (except closed Thur. pm and all day Fri.), Sun. 1400-1630.

Craignethan Castle Mar.-Oct., Mon.-Sat. 0930-1830 (except closed Thur. pm and all day Fri. in Mar. and Oct.), Sun. 1400-1830.

Doune Castle Apr.-Sep., Mon.-Sat. 0930-1830, Sun. 1400-1830.
Oct.-Mar., Mon.-Sat. 0930-1630 (except closed Thur. pm and all day
Fri.), Sun. 1400-1630.
Stirling Castle Apr.-Sep., daily 0930-1715. Oct.-Mar., daily 0930-
1615.

WESTERN ISLES

Kisimul Castle May-Sep., Mon., Wed., Sat. pm.

WEST LOTHIAN

Niddry Castle The castle is privately owned and open on summer
Sunday afternoons. Contact Edinburgh Tourist Information Centre for
details, tel. 0131 557 1700.